C. Pfoundes

Fu-So Mimi Bukuro

A Budget of Japanese Notes

C. Pfoundes

Fu-So Mimi Bukuro
A Budget of Japanese Notes

ISBN/EAN: 9783337166915

Printed in Europe, USA, Canada, Australia, Japan

Cover: Foto ©ninafisch / pixelio.de

More available books at **www.hansebooks.com**

FU-SO MIMI BUKURO.

A BUDGET

OF

JAPANESE NOTES,

BY

C. PFOUNDES.

REPRINTED FROM THE "JAPAN MAIL."

1875.

PRINTED AND PUBLISHED AT THE "JAPAN MAIL" OFFICE,
YOKOHAMA, JAPAN.

PREFACE.

The "Budget of Notes," now offered to the Public in a collected shape, has appeared from time to time in the columns of the *Japan Weekly Mail*, and forms a portion of the fruits of the compiler's research and study during a residence in this country already extending over more than a decade.

While unable to claim for them that they exhaust the vast field of enquiry in which they have been gathered, he ventures to hope that his notes may suggest to the younger student a range of subjects for deeper investigation, and that all may find in them an interesting record of a condition of things already beginning to pass away. The compiler would add that his information has been obtained from native authorities of assured trustworthiness and from actual observation.

It is intended to continue the issue of these "Notes," should the first part meet with a fair measure of encouragement.

Tokei, Japan,
    July, 1875.

TABLE OF CONTENTS.

	PAGES.
Superstitions	1
Charms	17
Household Altars and Gods	21
Musical Instruments	23
Native Literature	27
Poetry	29
Names	30
Street Signs	32
Dress	34
Beggars, Strollers and Vagabonds	36
Conveyances	38
Mons, or Crests	40
Childrens Schools	41
Sports	43
Female Accomplishments	48
Manly Accomplishments	51
Theatres	54
Pastimes	65
Music Teachers	73
Cosmogony	79
Religion	87
Buddhism	99
Buddhist Obsequies	134
Future State of the Buddhist	140
Hakama and *Kamishimo*	144
Suicide	147
Swords	158
Celebrated Swords and Makers	164
Names of Japan	171
Mythological and Legendary	173

扶 桑 耳 袋

FU SO MIMI BUKURO.

Superstitions.

A full description of the superstitions of any nation involves no easy task, and the delineation of those of such a nation as this, in such a manner as to enable the reader to realize their hold over the native mind, is more than we can expect to accomplish. In giving a sketch of some of the most common, we are only selecting exemplars from a thousand forms that are either local, temporary or of but slight consideration. An instructive and amusing essay on this subject might be written, which would throw no little light on the real depth of the religious feeling of the Japanese and of their capacity for entertaining a higher form of faith than any they now possess. There is a large class of young students growing up who sneer at any thing and everything native; but the great majority still resort, as did their ancestors, to all kinds of charms, prayers, incantations, amulets &c. to bring good luck, or ward off evil. In Shintooism, as we term it, there is but little room for superstition or ghost-stories, so that we are thrown upon the conclusion that the Buddhist priesthood are more or less the supporters of the gross follies which, in the form of superstitions, exist among all classes in this country.

Fortune-telling is much practised, and two forms of it are so common that they deserve a few words.

Oura-nai-sangi is practised with six pieces of hard wood marked in a prescribed manner; then with fifty-one pieces of bamboo like knitting-needles, of which one is laid down. The incantation is recited, the fifty are divided at random into two lots, one for each hand; these are then counted out into lots of eight each, and the odd ones left determine the order in which the sticks are to be placed. This is repeated twice, and the third time the standing needles *(medogi)* are counted out six at a time. The means by which the solution is ultimately arrived at is extremely complicated.

If a person, going to visit a sick friend or on other business, determines that the first word he hears accidentally of conversation between any strangers he meets coming towards him in the direction in which he is going, are to be omens of the friend's recovery or death, or of the success of the business, this method is called *tsujii-oura*.

Another kind of *tsujii-oura* is to have mottoes rolled up in pastry, in little bags of comfits, sugared peas or such sweet stuff, not unlike our style of bon-bon and cracker mottoes.

Girls try to divine the future by dropping a long hairpin from their head into the matting, and counting from the end of the pin, yes or no, yes—no, alternately, like Goethe's Margarethe as she pulls the leaves of the flower.

In building houses the lucky plan is to have the door to the south-east; the fire-proof store-room on the north-east; and the closets on the south-west,—the kitchen alongside of the store-room. There are, of course, means by which the necessity for this may be explained away when it is not convenient that the house should be thus built.

The best position for the *Kamidana* (shelf for the gods)—the household Buddhist altar;—where to place a temple to Inari Sama;—on what day to send the bride home;—when to set out on a journey, and so on, all have special rules to be observed, so that ill fortune may be avoided and success and prosperity ensured.

Physiognomy and palmistry are universally practised. These could not be described here without elaborate plates and explanations, but they could not be omitted from these notes. Launcelot Gobbo's "line of life" and "small trifle of wives," thus find their counterpart in Japan.

A box containing one hundred slips of bamboo, all numbered, is well shaken, and from a small hole in one end, one of the slips is shaken out. The number on this corresponds with the number of a paper on which the drawer's fate is written, often, it must be confessed, in the most ambiguous language.

Spirit-rapping in Japan has usually been practised by women. Their stock-in-trade consists of a small box (supposed to contain some mystery only known to the craft) of somewhat less than a foot square. It is said that, in the south, a dog is buried alive, the head only being left above ground, and food is then put almost within its reach, exposing it thus to the cruel fate of Tantalus. When in the greatest agony and near death, the head is chopped off and put in a box. To return, however. Only the craft know what the box really contains. The medium has also a small bow made of soft wood called *adzusa*, the string of which she twangs incessantly on the box, and a small cup of water placed in front of her, which is at the same time splashed out towards the enquirer. If the person to be 'interviewed' is living, a small piece of stick is used, and if a departed friend is to be summoned, a leaf from a grave-yard offering called *shikimi* is employed to splash the water out of the cup. The only question asked by the medium is whether the enquirer wishes to raise the dead or the living. Then after a half prayer, half incantation, the spirit commences to speak—through the medium. The mediums may be recognized by their invariably carrying, while out of doors, a small bundle of a peculiar shape, and also a light bark hat either on the head or in the hand.

Prayers for health or success in one's plans, for good fortune and so on, either by the priest of some *miya (kan-nushi)*, or the Buddhist priest of some shrine or temple, are still common, and innumerable as to form, place, and occasion.

Pilgrimages to Shintô and Buddhist shrines, from whence amulets, always exposed for sale there, are brought back, are very common. Such pilgrimages are made to numerous places, and every district has its own special place of resort, frequented by the devout or covetous. The places most generally visited by pilgrims from all the provinces and islands of Japan are *Fuji*, *Ise Dai Jin Gu*, *Sanuki Kompira*, *Musashi Suii Ten Gu* in Yedo, *Aki Miyajima*, *Shinano Zen kô jie*, each of which places will find mention elsewhere.

Men generally wear an amulet from Isé, besides those of local or special favourite shrines—the *bettoes*' (grooms) and servants' being suspended by a string round the neck. But gentlemen are ashamed of doing this and conceal them in some part of their dress, or in their tobacco-pouches and purses. Women carry their amulets in a girdle specially made for the purpose, and with which they never part for an instant except in the bath-house. Night and day it is on or near their persons. The most common amongst numerous others which swell the bundle to the dimensions of a good old-fashioned lady's bustle, are the *Kannon*, to give them ability and good fortune through life;—the *Gozo*, to bestow the gift of children and enable them to rear them;—the *Suii Tengu*, to save them from drowning and other harm, and, if choking, to swallow the paper of the amulet is a certain cure;—the figure of *Nichiren* and of *Kôbôdaishi*, to carry them to paradise;—*Sei-shɔ-ko*, for good luck;—*Benten*, for the gift of beauty, accomplishments and attractiveness to their lovers; *No se no Kuro fuda*, to save them from the wiles of the *kitsune* (fox); *Chiriu Gongen*—of San Shiu—to protect them from snakes, the greatest aversion of the Japanese woman;—*Aizen*, to cause her children to be loveable, and a host of others, local or selected for some special gift or power. Girls when very young have some of these suspended from the girdle in a small square pouch. Space does not admit of our enlarging further on this subject at present.

Ghosts and ghost-stories are innumerable and generally believed in. The greatest and most generally known Yedo ghost-story is that of *Kohada Kohejie,* an actor of the last century. His wife was unfaithful to him, and she and her lover wished to be rid of her husband. The lover took advantage of Kohada being on a tour in a provincial town, murdered him and returned to Yedo, to discover; however, that the ghost of his victim had preceded him, the ultimate consequence of Kohada haunting the guilty couple being, of course, the discovery of the crime.

An older tale than the foregoing is told of Oiewa, the wife of Tameya Iyemon of Yotzuya. Iyemon fell in love with his neighbour's daughter who was as beautiful as she was frail and criminal. By administering a potion which destroys beauty, and makes wives repulsive to their husbands, she contrived to disfigure Oiewa. Iyemon then treated his wife harshly and neglected her entirely now that she had ceased to attract and charm him. She bore him a child, but, after its birth, she became a maniac and destroyed it by biting its throat and died raving mad. Her ghost haunted the guilty pair, and killed the girl in the same way as Oiewa had killed her own child.

Sakura mura no Sogo (Sogo of the village of Sakura (cherries) in the province of Shimosa) is a tale well told elsewhere, of a farmer devoting himself for the good of his neighbours, and, by presenting a petition to the highest authorities asking protection against the injustice of his lord, incurring the death of himself and his family. His ghost haunted the *daimio* until he died a maniac.

Stories are told of women returning to this vale of woe to nurse the little ones they have unwillingly left behind.

If lovers are parted, and, while apart, are faithful, the one who dies first visits the remaining faithful one.

If a man passes at night the grave of some girl he has loved, and thinks of her, even though she had not reciprocated his affection, he is followed out of the grave-yard by a beautiful woman carrying a lantern. He recognizes her as his lost love, and she visits him every night afterwards in secret, until discovered by any third person. Any other living being than her lover can only see in her a ghastly skeleton, and the gifts or ornaments presented by her lover are afterwards found upon her tomb.

There is a story of a ghost appearing to an officer who lived near the present Engineering College. One of his favourite female attendants fell ill and was sent to her family to be nursed and cured. Subsequently she was reported to be hopelessly ill, and, on the very next day, to the surprise of her master's family, she made her appearance in the house, and reported herself as fit for duty, to commence which she said she would return on the morrow. On that evening the family heard of her having died at the hour when she was seen in her master's house. The master, a noted scoffer at ghost-stories and superstitions, became a firm believer in all at which he had previously mocked—so, at least, the story goes, as told us by our informer, a hearty believer in all such stories, though once a man in a very influential position.

A story is told of a *hatamoto* who had to exhibit his skill as an archer before the Shogûn, but who, being poor, arranged to borrow from a neighbour a quiver of arrows handsomer than his own. Just before the great day of the trial he sickened unto death, and, as his friend was deploring this misfortune, the supposed sick man called and borrowed the arrows, explaining away his unnaturally rapid recovery. A few days afterwards the lender heard that the borrower had died on the very day of the trial, and, upon visiting the grave, he found his beautiful and valuable arrows laid unharmed upon it.

Haunted spots are known and avoided. There is a tree on the moat opposite the Confucian College, there was one where the School of Languages now stands, and one near the spot where Iwakura was attacked about a year ago, all bearing a bad name, and on which the natives are said to have often found some of their countrymen hanging dead. In the last gasp before death, a green ball of fire is said to leave the body and take a wavy path, leaving a track behind it like a comet. If this is met with it may at times be caught by taking off the over-coat and throwing it over the ball of flame. The article of dress thus used for ever retains a strong and unpleasant odour. The act does not stay death, but only stays the passage of the soul.

When people die, the fluttering of birds, heard but unseen, in impossible places, and other peculiar sounds, re spoken of.

There is a way of raising a ghost, by putting into the lamp a hundred rush-lights, and, while reciting an incantation of a hundred lines, taking out one of the rush-lights as each line is finished; then go in the dark to a distant spot where a light is left burning and puff it out, when the ghost will appear.

Bake mono are ghosts of another kind, and not human, restless spirits. A girl named Okiku, the servant of a *hatamoto* living in the official quarter, about two centuries ago, accidentally broke a saucer, one of a valuable set of ten, made of some rare material and pattern, and said to have come from China in former times. Her master's anger, and his demand that she should replace the broken saucer, which she knew to be impossible, so frightened her, that she threw herself into a deep well in the garden. Ever afterwards her ghost came to count the saucers.

A ghost that appears to seamen always comes to borrow a dipper. If one with a bottom is given, the ghost bails water into the boat or junk and swamps it. One with the bottom knocked out is thrown overboard to prevent this catastrophe, and to be rid of the ghostly importunate. Gnomes, ghouls and goblins are as numerous in Japan as in all other countries where there are children to be frightened into quietness and obedience; and lazy, ignorant and worse than incapable and superstitious nurses or mothers to frighten their little charges, when they have lost control over their own patience and temper.

Mikoshi niudo is an immense bald-headed monster that lolls out his tongue, looking down over the tall folding screens. *Kakure zató* is a blind man with a staff who comes to carry bad people off to Hades. *Shitotsume kozo* is a one-eyed ghoul wearing a large hat, carrying in the hand a small sieve containing a ball of fire, the sight of which strikes terror into the beholder.

Rokuro-kubi. Some women are liable, while sound asleep and dreaming, to have their head leave their body, still slumbering, and roam about, the head only attached to the body by an almost imperceptible film. It is dangerous to arouse them till the head returns to its original position.

Gambari niudo is a ghoul that only appears on the new year's eve. When called thus, *Gambari nindo hoto to gisu,* a hairy hand is thrust forward, and if this can be seized and cut off it will bring wealth to the possessor.

Bake-mono tofu-uri (ghostly bean-cake seller) who goes about between midnight and morning. If met with, to speak to him brings evil consequences.

Ubume is a female spectre met with on river and canal banks and roads through marches, carrying a child. If met, she asks the traveller to favour her by holding the child for a few moments while she is absent. But after long and patient waiting the child becomes heavier and heavier, until it can be carried no longer, and then drops from the arms, a ponderous boulder which no man could lift.

Toori akuma. A story is told of this demon, that when a certain man was drinking *saké* on his verandah and enjoying the prospect before him, this hideous object appeared with a naked sword beyond the garden fence, and gradually seemed to float over it and towards the

the bibulous lord of his own house stretched at his ease. He hid himself under some carpeting, and from a sly corner spied the baffled demon making for his neighbour's house. The confusion next door soon attracted attention, and he discovered that his neighbour had attacked the demon with a naked sword, but had made the trifling mistake of chopping up his own wife, family and servants.

Hi no kuruma. This is a flaming wheel propelled by three demons, one green, one red and one black, all enveloped in flames, who come from Pandemonium for the bad people. These are seized when the measure of their iniquity is full, to ride on this fearful vehicle with its terrible charioteers, back to their home of raging fire.

Tengu is a demon who does not molest good people or his worshippers; but scoffers and scoundrels, beware! He is said to guard certain sacred places from sacrilege, especially some mountains and shrines consecrated to Kompira. He is invisible, but is represented in offerings to temples by a ruddy countenance and an enormous nose, and is generally accompanied by another mask, black, with an enormous beak; this latter is called *karasu tengu.* These two are called, first, the great nose is the *Dai Tengu*, representative of the male principle; the second, *Sho Tengu*, or beak, the female principle.

A celebrated writing-master of the early days of the century, went on a holiday trip to Nikko. Here he remained overnight at a place called Kobuga Hara, the house being the only one within some distance, occupied by Zenki Hayato. Now this Zenki was, as were his ancestors before him, the custodians of the Nikko *Tengu*. Our caligraphist saw with surprise an immense boiler of rice being emptied hot into an enormous tub, and taken to a room separate from the other apartments of the house, and, of course, his curiosity being excited, he asked why this was done. A little exercise of patience was recommended by his host, and, before long, loud and strange noises rather perturbed him, it being a lonely spot. A peculiar munching, crunching, smacking-of-lips kind of noise was next heard for some time, and then the scratching and scurrying he had first heard; then, dead silence. The host then took him to the room where the tub was, and not a single grain remained. The tub was scraped clean, and, with a solemn face and a warning sign, in a tone of awe, the host whispered "*Temmangu* has been to eat." The pedagogue durst not ask or say more.

The Fox and his pranks form the common and every-day burden to the tales of the marvellous, some of them no older than to-day or yesterday. Master *Kitsune* (fox) takes upon himself all shapes and forms, generally that of beautiful women, arrayed as occasion may require. In whatever shape, however, it always follows its victim, who consequently often falls into danger, such as over precipices, into rivers, wells, &c. Firm belief in the vagaries of this animal is not confined to any class, and no doubt he is painted blacker than he deserves, for he rarely troubles the fair sex.

A fox's wedding is a sight seen once in a life-time. It is conducted with all the pomp of the highest nobles of the land, and generally by torch-light and when there is no moon.

Foxes are supposed to steal away the senses of people, and to play practical jokes on them by no means amusing to their victims. For instance; to make them believe that a field of buck-wheat in flower is a river, and get them to strip and wade through it under that impression.—A young gentleman on a dreary wet day met a beautiful lady without an umbrella. Struck with her charms, he offered his own, and plied her ear with compliments. But he observed that her elegant robes were not in the slightest degree either damp or soiled, and were more suited to a fashionably assembly than to a walk on such a day. With a sudden effort he gathered himself together, and, with a prayer, drew his sword and made a fierce cut at the beauty. He then ran home and brought some followers to the spot, only to find a fine female fox badly wounded. While relating his story, he was asked how he knew that it was a fox, and he then told how he remarked the unsoiled robes, and became certain that the fox was trying to tempt him, when he saved himself by a huge effort. He subsequently made a pilgrimage and many votive offerings to protect him from further attempts of the family of the deceased.

The *Tanuki* (badger), unlike the fox, goes before his victims and these are generally women. He has the power not only of taking the shape of handsome loveable young men, but also of inanimate objects. A family formerly living near the Imperial College of Yedo was tormented by badgers, who frequently played jokes on the females of the household, sometimes appearing to the new serving-maids as an enormous tea-kettle.

A badger was once for a long time priest of the temple of Morinjie.

A waste-paper dealer once bought an iron pot for boiling water for tea, which he again sold, and on the purchaser placing it on the fire, a long tail and four legs appeared and away scampered the pot. This is the story Bumbuku-cha-maga.

Referring to the fox, we have overlooked some curious instances of this superstition. A story is told of a man who had trapped a fox being met by a poor man, who ransomed the beast and set it free. In the course of time, a beautiful girl appeared to the ransomer, and told him she was the fox whose life he had saved. Wishing to make him some return, the only way to do so would be by some pecuniary reward, which, for a fox, was an impossibility, but if the kind-hearted man would take her to one of the houses of public women and sell her there, he would be rewarded by the price without sin to himself. The poor man acted on this advice, and receiving a handsome sum in cash, returned joyfully to his home in the mountains. The fox after playing many tricks on the people of the house and practical jokes on her admirers, disappeared in the garden as a fox. Of course the people of the house never recovered the money. Thus the good were rewarded and the wicked got their deserts.

About fifty years ago, a fox, notorious for its mischievous propensities, lived in one of the suburbs of Yedo called Honjo, and an officer of the Tokugawa household boasted that he was smart enough to fool the fox. Seeing a large fox, as he thought, asleep one day in the locality reputed to be frequented by our sly renard, the officer cried out "Oh, sister, don't sleep there, you will catch cold; come along!" The fox awoke, and following the officer, took the shape of his sister. He then invited the former to a restaurant where they had the best of everything spread before them. On some trivial pretext the officer left the room and sent the attendants thither, when they were horrified to see an enormous old fox greedily attacking all the edibles. A general assault was made on him, but he escaped. The officer returned and told the joke he had played on the fox, hoping that it had been killed, or at least caught. But the fox had the best of it, for the officer had to pay the reckoning!

Many stories are told about cats. The following is a fair specimen.

In a certain high officer's residence in Yedo some thirty years ago, a female attendant named *Osode* (sleeve) was sewing one evening and heard her name called two or three times. Looking round she only saw a cat well known in the house. Again and again she was called, and at last concluded that the voice must come from the cat. Pussy then asked for the loan of a kerchief, a request with which Osode complied, out of curiosity to see the result. In thanking her, the cat told her that if she would look out of one of the closet windows into the garden where the moon threw its brightest rays, after the rest of the household had gone to rest, she would see an amusing sight. Osode, as well as the other members of the household, having retired, she cautiously stole out to the spot named, and, to her astonishment, saw the cats of the neighbourhood collected together, holding what is called in Australia a "Corroboree," each cat dressed in a kerchief and dancing away at a fine rate. Next morning she privately informed the master of this, and was ordered to let him know the next time Puss asked for anything. In a few days the cat wished again to borrow a kerchief, when Osode, by a preconcerted signal, called her master, who rushed into the room with a lance. But too late; Puss had vanished! In spite of all search along the road of escape she could not be found. The only peculiarity observed was a patch of plaster on one of the roads as if lately repaired. The master struck at this with his lance, and behold Puss impaled! A horn was found on the cat's forehead and was cut off and preserved.

Another story is told of a *hatamoto* family during the early part of the present century.

While the master was away on official business, his wife was taken ill. He had some time previously adopted a young man as his son, and in honour of this son's approaching marriage a feast was arranged. On the day of the feast the sick woman recovered. Just before the fish and other good things were spread before the assembled guests, certain fish were missed under such suspicious circumstances as to draw attention to the till now sick woman. The result of strict search was to find the body of the sick woman under the verandah partly devoured, and the apparently recovered patient was dispatched with a rapid sweep of the young man's sword, leaving only the carcase of a cat.

Kappa is a monster inhabiting certain rivers, and takes upon itself either the form of a child or some article likely to drop into a river. In trying to recover this object the *kappa* steals the victim's soul.

Otters take on themselves the forms of hobbledehoys and appear to women and play pranks.

CHARMS.

Every country has its peculiar superstitions which cling with a force that even education fails completely to remove. It can therefore furnish no matter for surprise that they should be all-powerful among a people so peculiarly susceptible to their influence as the Japanese. Pilgrimages to certain well-known localities are very commonly undertaken by believers for purposes of prayer and of making offerings, be it at ancient trees, stones or shrines, of pictures, sprinklings of salt or old sandals, each possessing its reputation as a specific for some physical or mental malady. If, on the 8th day of the 4th month, a certain grass known as *pen pen gusa* be gathered and hung within the paper lanterns, it is said to protect the possessor from insects. An incantation is also used which, however, is untranslateable. If the dew on the grass be gathered on the 1st day of the 5th month it will cure sores on the feet. Farmers believe, that if they attach a *namako* (beche-de-mer) to a string and draw it round their fields the moles will desert them. Seven of the small red beans named *azuki* for males, and double that number for females, if swallowed with water on new year's day, are a prophylactic against disease. If a small spot above each ear be left unshaven on the heads of young children they will be secured against a scrofulous disease of the scalp. If a traveller before undertaking a journey, be it on horse-back, ship, vehicle or chair, writes the character *shin* (red) on the palm of his left hand and licks it off he will be preserved from harm. If a tiresome visitor causes inconvenience by the length of his call, the broom is inverted, a towel thrown over it, and the supposed effigy is energetically fanned. Should this charm fail to effect its purpose moxa is applied to the visitor's clogs or sandals. In order to produce dreams of an absent friend or lover, it is recommended to turn the sleeves of the bed-quilt to the foot of the bed.

The rice boiler is said to vibrate with such violence at times as to give forth a loud humming noise. If this begins faintly and grows afterwards stronger it is said to indicate good luck; if loudly, the reverse is predicted, but in such cases it should at once be stopped by enveloping it in the under-clothing of a female, a virgin if possible. It is believed that a bean dropped into the well for each day a journey is supposed to last, will preserve the traveller's feet from foot-sores. In order to secure fine weather for any proposed journey, girls make a figure of paper known as *teri-teri-boz*, which they suspend by a piece of thread to a tree of the belladonna species, called *naruten*. After making offerings of rice and throwing *saké* over it, they set it adrift in the nearest stream.

To prevent an offensive odour from cesspools, it is recommended to fill a tea-cup with water, and placing a tray over it, to invert both. If in this movement none of the water is spilled, the charm should have taken effect.

It is believed that if *amé* (candy) be rubbed upon scrofulous sores on the body, and then placed upon a *yênoki* tree, a cure may be depended on. A horse's tooth, if rubbed upon pimples on the face, is thought to remove them. The gridiron used for broiling fish is held above the head and thrice turned as a charm to prevent the fish from adhering to the metal. Good luck at lotteries is thought to be obtained by removing the tops of the laths from graves, or the pumice-stone employed at the public baths for rubbing down the horny parts of the feet.

Witchcraft.

Jealous women employ this charm to avenge the infidelity of their husbands or lovers. Dressing herself in white, her hair hanging loose behind, a tripod (usually one of those used in cooking) on which three lighted candles are placed, on her head, while in her mouth she holds a torch of bamboo and pine roots lighted at both ends, and round her neck a mirror, the slighted fair rises at the hour of the Bull (about 2 A.M.) and taking an effigy of the faithless one, or, as the case may be, of his frail companion or of both, nails it to a tree within the grounds of some shrine. At whatever part of the effigy the nail is driven, there will injury be inflicted upon the original in the flesh, but if she should meet the ghost of an enormous bull and exhibit terror at the apparition, the potency of the charm is lost, and can only be revived with incantation and imprecations on the offending pair. The common mode of bewitchment is to form a lay figure of straw, pierced with nails, and to bury it beneath the place where the person to be punished usually sleeps.

Amulets and other charms are very numerous, and the entrance gates of private residences or the fronts of townspeople's houses are covered with numerous specimens. Each family has its patron saints and favourite *kami*, for whom labels are periodically provided for a trifling fee; but the members of the family who make pilgrimages, which are as a matter of fact mere excuses for holiday excursions, return provided with tickets from the places they have visited. These are for Yedo: *Tomioka Hachiman; Fugiko; Naritano Fonda; Hori no Uchi Soshi; Dai Shi; Nikko Gongen; Aki Ha*, to which a host innumerable of others may fairly be added.

A piece of paper bearing the impression of a black hand is employed to ward off an attack of small-pox. This is the hand of *Chinsei-hachiro-tami-tomo*. A piece of red paper with three of the characters for ' horse ' serves a similar purpose. A rice spoon is also used. Garlic is hung up to protect sufferers from chills and colds.

Household Altars and Gods.

Every house, be it poor or rich, possesses a *Kamidana*, or shelf for the gods. On this is placed the *Tenshokodaijingú*, a small box containing the *miya* (temple) which is brought each year from the province of Isé. The box is formed of thin chip and paper and contains the *Go-hei* together with a small piece of bamboo. The *Go-hei* is a religious symbol, and is formed of strips of paper cut in a particular shape and bearing the inscription "Ten Thousand Prayers." Besides these, each family holds its especial divinities in honour and brings home from the *miyas*, or from other pilgrimages, tickets which are placed upon the same shelf. These are innumerable. Fixed days are assigned for offering up the *fuda*, when paper ornaments and rice cakes are deposited with them. These days are the 1st, 15th and 18th days of each month; the five great holidays viz. the 3rd day of the 3rd month, 5th day of the 5th month, 7th day of the 7th month, 9th day of the 9th month and the *Toshi-koshi*, or last day of winter, an uncertain period before the revision of the calendar.

A *Butzu-dana*, (or Buddha shelf) is to be found in every house, notwithstanding the remarkable growth of religious scepticism among the student class. This is the household altar, and the memorial tablets of departed relatives are deposited thereon. A record is kept of the anniversaries of decease of members of the family, and on these days special prayers in their favour are recited. A priest is frequently employed for this purpose. In addition to the figure of *Amida-nuirai*, the *Tendai* sect place a representation of *Gan-san-dai-shi*, their founder, upon their household altars.

The *Shin-gon* join the representation of *Kobo-dai-shi* to that of *Amida*.

The *Iko-shiu* honour in like manner their founder *Shin-ran-sho-nin*.

The *Zen-shiu* add *Daruma-dai-shi*, their founder, to the figure of *Amida*.

The *Nichi-ren-shiu* have *Amida* and *Taho-nuirai*, separated by a pillar which bears the prayer *Na-mu-mio-no-ren-gei-kio*, written thereon in seven Chinese characters, and in addition to these *Nichiren-dai-bu-satzu*, the founder of this sect.

The *Joodo* sect honour their founder *Enko-dai-shi*.

The *Ko-jin-dana*, or shelf for the god of the kitchen, may also be found in the kitchens. In honour of this god offerings of pictures of poultry and pine-branches are made at the end of every month. At all of these shelves oil lights are lighted during the period of family devotions, morning and evening.

The owners of land formerly dedicated small temples in their domains to *Inari*, god of the soil. His chief temple is situated at Kioto (now Sai Kio), and as the hill upon which it is built formerly sheltered large numbers of foxes, we find this animal commemorated at every temple, however small, by figures of foxes carved in stone and placed on either side.

Musical Instruments.

The instrument most commonly met with in Japan is the *samisen* ("the three pleasant-sounding strings,") and no girl is considered educated who does not possess some knowledge of it. There are three methods in which this instrument is tuned: the *hon-chôshi*, or true; the *ni-agari*, or second-raised; and the *san-sagari*, or third-lowered. There is also the *taka-ne* or sound raised, used when more than one *samisen* is being played in company, thus constituting in fact first and second. The pupils are instructed according to a variety of methods known as *Joruri*. These are the *Gidaiyu*; *Tomi-moto*; *Tokiwazu*; *Kiyomoto*; *Kishisawa*; *Nagauta*; *Itchiubushi*; *Katobushi*; *O-satzuma*; *Sonohachibushi*; *Outazawa*; *Haouta* and *Shinnai*. Of these a few of the last-named are now seldom taught nor is instruction usually imparted in more than one school, the formation of the voice necessary for any one of the methods rendering it difficult to follow others. Copious notes on this subject will be found elsewhere.

There is a considerable difference in the sizes in which this truly national instrument is made, and most makers possess certain peculiarities which distinguish their manufacture. The *Joruri samisen* is larger and thicker than a *Nagauta samisen*. The maker of highest repute is named Koomi, and his finest instruments are made of *karin* and *sh'tan*. They are covered with catskin, its special adaptability for the purpose being determined by the number of nipples on the skin which mark the animal's age. The three strings are of various sizes, depending upon the description of the instrument, and are made of silk which is spun hard and coated with glue. The instrument is played with a *bachi,* or piece of shaped ivory, and the bridge is made of bamboo, though frequently also of ivory, horn, or tortoiseshell.

The *Koto,* which corresponds to the European harp, is a long box over which thirteen strings about five feet long are stretched. The styles of playing are known as *Yamada, Yamase,* and *Ikuta.* It is tuned according to the *Hira-choshi,* which is the more common method, or the *Kumoi,* the latter being taught only to the more advanced pupils. This instrument is rarely played by men, but a class named *kengio* (blind men) used formerly to perform upon it, and blind instructors may even now be occasionally met with. The *koto* is made of a light and soft wood named *kiri.* The bridges—of which there is one to each string—are formed of hard-wood and ivory, and the strings which are of silk, are of an uniform length but varying in thickness. The tuning is effected by shifting the position of the bridges from the end of the instrument at the right hand, farther for the low notes and nearer for the high Semi-tones are obtained by pressing the string with the left hand behind the bridges as it is struck. The right hand thumb and first and second fingers are armed with long artificial nails with which the strings are sounded. The singing accompaniments are the *omote* (or outside) *naka* (or inside) *oku* (or retired) and the *sahumono.*

The *Biwa* resembles a flat mandoline with four strings. It is commonly employed to accompany the *Hei-ki-mono-*

gatari and is more used by priests than by women. Murákami Tennô, one of the former Emperors, was extremely partial to this instrument on which he was an expert performer. He received from Morokoshi (China) the Ken-jo, Sei-zan, and Shishi-maru, these three being pre-eminently fine instruments.

The *Kokiu* is a small *samisen*, played with a bow, and is generally used to accompany the latter and the *koto*. It is, however, not much played by the lower classes.

Of the *Fuye*, or flute, there are many kinds, known as the *otcki, nokan, shinobuye* and *kusabuye*.

Of drums there are *kayen no tyco* (war drums), *kagura* (large and small varieties) and *shime-daiko*. These are played with sticks of dimensions varying according to circumstances.

Tsudzumi is a kind of drum. The *Kakko* is played with long thin sticks. *No* and *Shibai* (old and new) are played, one held up in the left hand and one under the same arm, in which position they are beaten with the right hand. They are employed to accompany the *samisen*.

Shô is an instrument of eight reeds, played with four fingers of each hand. It is but little used, and only as an accompaniment to other instruments.

Shak-hatchi and *Shitoyogiri* consist of a straight tube, usually of bamboo, about eighteen inches in length and one and a-half inches inside diameter; one half of the upper edge being cut off sharp. It is weak in tone and possesses but a slight range. One of its most elaborate *morceaux* is styled *Tsuru-no-sugomori.* This instrument was used by the *komoso* class.

Hichiriki resembles our clarionet and is used to accompany other instruments on such occasions as Shintô Festivals or a Court Fête.

Odori (Dancing or Posturing.)

By *Odori* may be understood the arts of *pose* and gesture to the accompaniment of musical instruments. Its *riugi,* or distinctive modes of execution, are known as *Fujima, Nishigawa, Hanayagi, Midzuki, Nakamura, Iwai, Sawamura,* and at theatres when the posturing is unaccompanied by music, *Furi-ts'ke.* The accomplishment is usually imparted to girls at a very tender age, and children of only four or five years old may be observed at their lessons, with rouged lips and a streak of *beni* at the corners of the eyes and on the lobes of their ears; head partially shaved, and the remaining locks tortured into fantastic shapes by the aid of hair-pins and gold or coloured ribands.

They subsequently receive lessons in posture from singing girls of reputation in their art, and when more advanced are instructed by skilled actors.

Native Literature.

The Japanese possess a copious literature and have as a nation a strong predilection for reading, which the ample time at the disposal of most classes affords abundant opportunity for indulging. Their catalogues of published works are both numerous and voluminous and class the native books in the following subdivisions:

Kan-gaku, or Chinese Classical Literature and works on the subject. In this class may be included books upon Buddhism (*Butzusho*) written in Chinese, as well as the commentaries on these and the form of verse known as *shi* by native authors.

Wa-gaku, or native works upon exclusively Japanese subjects, such as history, geography, books upon subjects of local interest, art and old poetical tales *(yomi uta)*, &c.

Kesaku, or novels, tales, and historical events worked up into romances. Of this class they possess a boundless variety, and many of their circulating libraries are principally formed of these books. Among the older of their staple writers are Kiosan, the Japanese "Swift"; Kioden, the "Smollett"; *Ikku*, the humourist who wrote the *Hisa-kure-ge;* Samba, a comic writer whose works resemble our Thackeray in his "Book of Snobs"; Hokuba, a writer of Ghost-Stories, Fairy Legends, Tales of Bewitchment and of inanimate objects being endowed with life and speech, &c., &c.

The writers of later times are: Bakin, whose tales embody real names and descriptions, and who professed to render them vehicles of moral teaching. The scene of some of his stories is laid in China. He may be styled the "Scott" of Japan. Tanehiko, a contemporary of Bakin, flourished during the last generation. His chief work "*Inaka Genji*" a story pourtraying the times in which he lived, and which was written not long before the opening of the country to foreign intercourse, furnishes an admirable description of the mode of life of the various classes at a recent period. Tanehiko was a small *hatamoto*, and the composition of the work we have named procured him his degradation by the Government. He was reputed to possess considerable ability as author of tales from the native stage which are known as *Shohon-jitate*. The works of Tamenaga Shinsui, which chiefly consist of novels and love tales, are held in considerable estimation by his countrymen. Being modern compositions they afford fair specimens of the production of writers of this class at the present day. The Authors of Legends, Travels, Tales of Folk-Lore &c. swell the list of littérateurs to no mean length. Each year sees copious additions to the monstrous catalogue of literary productions, and gives much cause to wish that a judicious censorate were in existence. One class of this garbage, which we can only here allude to, is happily dying out, but it is said that one volume of it at least is reputed to confer good luck when kept among the dresses of females.

POETRY.

The long poetry is formed of sentences of seven and five syllables alternately. Short poetry consists of thirty-one syllables only in *kami-no-ku*, the first sentence comprising five syllables, the second seven, the third five, and the fourth and fifth seven syllables each. These are frequently written on long and narrow slips of ornamented card-board, 14 inches long and $2\frac{9}{10}$ inches in breadth, which are called *tanzaku*.

Honka is another variety, the syllables following in the same order, but read differently. *Zootoka* has the same number of syllables. These are, however, so formed as to demand a poetical reply of the same order. *Seidooka* possesses a similar syllabic order and formation, but the beginning and end consist of words or characters of like meaning.

Kioka are the ordinary poems of thirty-one syllables in the same order.

Omugayashi is similar to *zootoka* with the exception that the two verses, question and reply, have only one of the thirty-one syllables different. In the change of this the merit of the performance consists.

Oriku are acrostics of thirty-one syllables, divided into lines of five and seven syllables twice alternating and ending in one of seven syllables. The first syllable or character of each line is given arbitrarily.

Haikai is of the same number and order of syllables,

but is simply a poetical play on words, or, it may be, a proverb.

Renga is the *kami-no-ku* or verse of five, seven and five syllables answered by the *shimo-no-ku* of seven and seven syllables, the whole forming a poem of thirty-one. *Hai kai* is similar to *renga*, though commonly employed upon more trivial subjects. Both are called *tzukeai* (or joining).

Hokku is the five, seven and five, or seventeen syllable poem.

Sen-riu has five, seven and five syllables. It is a *jeu de mots*.

Names.

The Japanese tradesman, unlike the Chinaman, is not accustomed to adopt high-sounding titles to denote his place of business and, until recently, tradesmen were designated by the names of their respective stores to which their own surnames were added. Their business signs, or trade-marks, as we should style them, reproduced in many cases the names of the province from which the family originally came, to which frequently their former trade was added. Thus, presuming Kane-Ko (metal child) to be carrying on business in Mito Ya (Mito's shop), his trade designation would be Mito Ya Kane-ko. Of late all classes are permitted to use a surname, a privilege confined in former days to the official class. These surnames evidently derive their origin from the names of the landed property of those who bear them. We find among them the names of woods, forests, underwood, quick-river, hill-town, cliff-bridge, cliff-cape, front field, small stream, virtuous river, river-mouth, or other words usually compounded of two Chinese characters, names of one or three forming the exceptions. It is permitted to families to bestow their surnames on persons not related to them, and in this manner the nobility was accustomed to honour its retainers, and the *samurai* the servants and tradesmen who lived under their protection.

Besides the surname, or family designation, the Japanese employ the common name which corresponds with our baptismal title, and a preference is shown by some families for names possessing certain peculiarities, as, for example, Yoshitaro, Yoshigiro, Yoshisaburo, Kitchi-(or Yoshi-)noske. The eldest son's bestowed name frequently ends in Taro, the second son's in Gi and the third in Saburo. Grandsons who use the same name as their fathers and grandfathers embody the character *mago* (grandson) and great-grandsons the character *hiko*. The son, on reaching manhood, has a name chosen for him which usually expresses some hoped-for quality or good fortune. This is the name used by officials.

Azana is a *nom de plume*, employed by students or literary men.

Go is a fancy name, adopted chiefly by those who retire from active life, or who prefer to be known among their friends under some other than their ordinary title.

Kai mio is the posthumous name which is engraved upon the tomb-stone. This is usually selected by the priests, and is determined by certain rules varying according to the sect and rank of the deceased.

Women have no surnames. They are known by a name *(yobi na)* which is selected by the parents about a week after the birth of the infant. The names of fruits, trees, flowers, colours, birds, certain animals, or some other fancy name selected arbitrarily, usually furnish this designation which, except when the person is addressed by a parent or superior, is generally used with the prefix O. The names of singing and dancing girls are frequently elaborated by the addition of qualifying words, as, for instance, *Ko yoshi* (the little fortune), while those of the public women are still more fancifully adorned, thus: *Fujinami* (the waves of the wisteria blossom.)

The daughters of the upper classes usually receive a name on their betrothal which consists of one Chinese character. It is chosen by their friends, but is very rarely used.

The *Kai mio* is the only other name given to women. This is posthumous as in the case of males.

Street Signs.

Although the gorgeous ornamentation which characterises the street signs of the Chinese tradesman are not met with in this country, each trade is nevertheless represented by its distinctive and peculiar symbol.

A cluster of cypress, trimmed into spherical shape, and varying from one to two feet in diameter, furnishes the ancient *saké*-shop sign. It is also customary to place the young twigs of this tree in the bung-holes of the kegs or in the mouths of the bottles, the spines being downwards. The prickly spines are said to ward off insects and to keep the *saké* sweet. The hatters suspend a long string of hats from their shops, and the ׅmaccaroni-dealers affix to their shop-fronts a large paper lantern which enumerates the name of the house, the edibles it will supply and their price per bowl. The original price was two pieces of 8 *mon* or .008 parts of a Mexican dollar.

Hosiers employ a sign which represents one side of a stocking, which is so made as to allow of the great toe being separate from the others. *Beni Ya*, the sellers of crimson cosmetic for painting women's lips, exhibit a small crimson flag. *Sushi Ya*, the purveyors of small rolls of rice and fish, furnishing each about two mouths-full—the Japanese sandwich in fact—use a flag with their house name, and an enumeration of the various articles they prepare : *matz* (pine) ; *misago*, so called from a fishing-bird ; *kenuki* (boned fowl) and *inari* are a few of these names.

Wrestlers write their names on a board. Theatres exhibit representations of the most telling scenes in the piece being played. Herbalists and druggists display monstrous bags, resembling in shape the small ones used in infusing the medicines. Makers of rosaries suspend a large rosary from their shops. Gold-beater's signs, unlike the enormous, gilt arm which indicates the craftsman in European countries, are pairs of large square spectacles, the space for the glasses being filled up with sheets of gold leaf.

A sign may be observed composed of two *tai* (Serranus

M.), the fish being coloured red and represented as if tied together by the gills with straw. This is usually exhibited by dealers in dried and salt fish, eggs, &c., and is employed to denote that the shop can supply the usual presents to betrothed persons. Sellers of cut-flowers plant a willow tree at one corner of their houses. Retail tea-dealers exhibit a small jar, and lacquer men a chip box, used to contain lacquered-ware. Tobacconists display their names and trade-marks on a reddish-brown strip of cloth hung up in front of their shops. Workers in hair show a small octagon box with a fringe of hair hanging from it. Kite-makers use as a sign a cuttle-fish, both kite and fish being known as *tako*. *Ama*, or sweet-*saké* dealers exhibit a painting of Fujiyama.

Many other signs, as may be imagined, are employed by the Japanese shopkeepers to illustrate the nature of their occupations. To explain a large number of these would require the use of Chinese characters and a literal full-length interpretation, and this would demand much time and much space.

Japanese Dress.

To each class of the Japanese population a special description of clothing is assigned, varying in material according to season. These may be divided into the ordinary, festive, mourning, professional, official, state and other special fashions of dress. The labourer, farmer and handicraftsman do not overburden themselves with clothing :—a loin-cloth forms their light summer raiment, while their cold-weather costume is usually comprised in wrapper and short girdle. The better class of artisan and shopkeeper wear a *haori*, or short dress, over all, when out of doors, and from the thinnest gauze which they wear in the heat of summer they change in succession to single cotton cloth, to lined cotton, and finally, to cotton-wadded garments in winter, silk clothing being reserved for festivals, visits, or great occasions.

Firemen wear thickly padded and quilted dresses with mittens and caps which match them. Small officials and many of the better class of tradesmen use the *hakama*, or split petticoat, the dress being tucked into it and the *haori* worn over all. On special occasions, and in place of the *haori*, an upper dress, resembling a pair of wings, hangs from the shoulders. It is formed of a material resembling the *hakama* worn with it, but is seldom seen at present.

The *hakama* and *haori* are worn by the *samurai* class, and on special occasions the *kami shimo*, or winged jacket. The ordinary dress of the Daimios resembled the foregoing somewhat. To describe it worthily will demand a special chapter.

The dress of females of the lower and middle classes differ only in the quality of material, the fashion of all being alike.

In the national mode of dressing the hair, now falling into disuse, the locks are gathered to the crown of the head, tied there, and the *queue* carried over to the forehead, a patch being kept clean shaven on which it rests.

Beggars, Strollers and Vagabonds.

Beggars may usually be seen in large numbers in the approaches to the temples on the chief festival days. Here may be met the lame, halt and blind, lepers, and deformity in some of its most hideous phases. The beggars accompany their prayers for the charitable with a hideous noise, which they make by striking little metal discs or battledores of raw hide that they carry. The beggar frequently takes his stand on bridges, or near running streams, where he importunes the passer-by to purchase live eels or other fish, and to perform the devout work of releasing them as prescribed by Buddhist doctrine.

Among strollers we find the *shishi* (or lion.) This is a representation of a lion's head, with a moveable underjaw and a flowing mane, fitted on to a capacious skirt beneath which the man is concealed who works it. The "lion" is accompanied by two men, one performing on a small cylindrical drum and a triangle, and the other playing a flute from which they extract excruciating music. The capacious mouth of the lion is supposed to swallow the evil spirits who may be attracted by his gambollings and the accompanying music. *Saru mawashi* are a class of strollers who take about with them performing monkeys. *Saru-ya machi* (monkey-shop-street) is their head quarters in town. It is related that in years gone by when the favourite horse of a famous warrior fell sick and was about to die, it was restored to health by a monkey who possessed a curative charm. Since this incident occurred until a few years ago, it was customary to amuse the horses in the government stables on new year's days by a visit of the performing Court monkeys, an example which was generally followed by the nobility. Female monkeys only are trained to perform.

Street tumblers and athletes are, with one exception, unworthy of notice. This exception is the wrestler, who, nearly naked, represents a wrestling bout, appearing to be struggling with an invisible opponent, and assuming the attitude of overcoming or being overcome by him.

The *Sai-mon* were originally travelling preachers. They are now begging story-tellers. They hold in their hands a jingling toy upon which they strike. The *Tsuji-go-shaku* are the lecturers who may be observed seated on some vacant piece of ground, sheltered by mats. They relate the deeds of prowess of the popular heroes, and may be always seen surrounded by a crowd of listeners. The *Kowaiero* recites scenes from famous dramas, imitating as far as possible the tones of celebrated actors. The *Shinnai* accompany their stories with a performance on the *samisen*.

Yashi include sellers of quack medicines, dealers in spice and incense, ballad singers and sellers and hawkers of the latest express news, recounting the last reported murder, fire, robbery or scandal. *Onna daiyu* are women of the Yeta class. They wear large sun-hats and earn a scanty subsistence by playing and singing at the house doors. Blind women (*goze*,) may also be met singing to a *samisen*. They used formerly to be supplied by the Government with passes which insured them a night's lodging when on their travels.

In the early days of the Tokugawa dynasty, it is

related, four priests arrived in Yedo from the south bearing a petition to the Government. Their prayer was not granted nor was its tenour made public, but a ward of the city known as Hashimoto chô was assigned to them as a residence, and they were placed under the protection of the *Ouyeno-no-mia-sama*. It has been supposed that their object was to originate a new *Shiumon* (religious sect) and to this day their followers are known as *Gan-nin-boz* (priest-petitioners). Admission to this sect is often sought for by very poor persons. The sect is not recognised and possesses no temples, but it holds itself aloof from all others.

Pilgrims, who during the period of their pilgrimage are known as *Jun rei*, are to be met on the roads at all seasons clad in white cotton. They are chiefly of the farming or artisan class who hope to earn dispensations by their pilgrimages. They have to visit sixty-six of the numerous shrines of Kuannon (known to Europeans as the Buddhist goddess of mercy) which are scattered throughout this Empire.

Conveyance.

The mode of conveyance formerly employed by the Court at Kioto was the bullock cart. They also used a chair of state, hung on two poles and borne upon the shoulders of four carriers. The Daimios used a form of palanquin slung on a long pole and carried by several men who walked before and behind. Physicians travelled in *kagos*, smaller vehicles than the foregoing, but borne by means of long poles. Townspeople used the *Ampotsu kago,* which was shaped like that of the physicians but with sliding doors and a shorter pole. The usual pack-*kago* for hire in the streets was furnished with a mat, hanging down on either side. *Yama kago* (hill chairs) were made of bamboo basket-work and were so light when laden as to be borne by two or three men.

Boats of all descriptions are in use, ferry, river, and seagoing, and pleasure boats, roofed or otherwise. To these and to the passenger boats of the Inland Sea we shall take some future opportunity to recur.

Sledges are furnished with wooden runners and are drawn up or eased down hill by ropes. They are usually only employed in the hilly country in winter. Fordable rivers are crossed on wooden platforms, borne on men's shoulders. Prisoners are conveyed about in bamboo cages. Only entire horses are used for the saddle, mares being never ridden and but seldom employed for packing purposes. They are rarely seen in the towns, and geldings are absolutely unknown. The Government had formerly its breeding establishments at Kogane in Shimosa and at Ashidaka in the neighbourhood of Fujiyama. The Sendai (Northern province) horses have always been held in excellent repute in Yedo, and large numbers of them are bred and brought to the metropolis for sale in the autumn.

Mons (or Crests.)

The *Bushi* originated the custom of using crests. Of old each bore his device upon his banner, armour and other property; and as it was deemed a high honour for a retainer that he should be permitted to wear his master's crest, the practise extended in course of time and has finally become general.

The *Kiku* (chrysanthemum) and a leaf named *Kiri* (Paulonia) are appropriated exclusively by the Imperial family.

The *Mitzu aoie* (somewhat resembling the shamrock and consisting of three leaves in a circle), forms the blazon of the Tokugawa family, and is said to have been adopted by them when Chikuami retired to the province of Mikuni, where, at the village of Sakaimura, he was presented with cakes laid upon three similar leaves. In honour of the event the family adopted this as their cognisance. Matzudaira Tarozaiemon, who adopted Chikuami, lived near the village, and when his family and that of Sakai were subsequently incorporated as one, the name Tokugawa was selected and the *kata-bami-kusa* became the crest of their descendants.

Family crests are innumerable, each family using several in addition to their hereditary devices. Women vary the mode of wearing their crests according to the dictates of taste, placing them between the shoulders and at the back part of the sleeves of their garments. Sometimes the first of these alone is worn, sometimes all three, and in some cases two more, one on each sleeve in front, are added. The device worn by members of the family is usually of a size smaller than a florin, the retainers, on the other hand, using a crest larger than a crown-piece. Chair-bearers, *bettos* and other menials commonly wear some portion of the crest or other well-known family cognisance to distinguish them; while houses, gateways, roof-tiles and all the miscellaneous paraphernalia of the family—from its rain-coats and umbrellas to the finest lacquer-ware—are invariably marked with the distinctive family badge. Merchants add their trade marks to other distinguishing devices.

Children's Schools.

Children are rarely sent to school before their seventh year—according to the Japanese mode of reckoning age—(between the fifth and sixth year according to ours) and boys and girls in the infant-schools receive their instruction together.

A lucky day is chosen—the usual time is the beginning of the second month,—the scholar takes a present to the teacher, and also cakes for his school-fellows, his parents or relatives providing the usual pencils, paper, desk, inkstone &c. The first lesson is the *I, Ro, Ha*, in the vulgar *hirakana*, the numerals, the names of persons, countries, cities &c of Japan, in the order imparted. This is the introductory *Tei narai* (hand learning) or writing-school course. To this succeeds the study of the *sho-soku-ôrai*. The studies of girls generally conclude with the *Onna-Ima-Gawa,* and *Hia ku-Nin-I-Shiu*—a verse from each one of a hundred poets.

The *Onna Dai Gaku* (Female Great Learning), a work of greater pretension prepared for young ladies of more advanced powers and greater capacity, follows this, and a few kindred works which can hardly be called school-books. Boys are taught to write the Chinese characters from the *San-ji,* and combinations of three characters; then the *Dô-ji-kio,* a child's book; next, the *Dai Gaku* (Great Learning) of Confucius. The Chinese classics follow and the boys' memory of the eye for Chinese characters is fully exercised, but no more.

School holidays in the olden time, and before the introduction of foreign professors *ad libitum,* were on the 1st, 15th and 25th of each month. Before the latter day, called *Ten jin ko,* the pupil brought the monthly contribution to the teacher, and a copy, to show by comparison with the last, the progress made. Then there is the quarterly copy written without the *Te hon* (original hand-guide) or copy.

The half-yearly exhibition is a great event, a day for the display of best clothes, and the enjoyment of good things in the form of cakes, fruit &c, paid for of course by the friends of the pupils, who have also to make donations to the teacher in winter for providing charcoal to warm the school-room.

The boys and girls are separated, the girls remaining near the teacher, while the boys are placed nearer the door. Or, if there is an up-stairs room, the bigger boys are sent there in charge of the assistant teacher or pupil-teacher.

School parties and picnics generally demand that the pupils be dressed alike, especially the girls, who, in addition to the writing-school, attend singing, dancing and music teachers. The wealthy alone can afford to have their daughters taught at home.

Children's Sports.

Girls in Japan have their dolls, doll-houses, and toys and toy kitchen utensils, from the simplest and cheapest. to the most expensive and elaborate, according to the extent of their pocket-money. Little ladies are to be seen, as in other countries, mimicking their elders. Toy theatres, usually painted on paper, cut out, and glued into the proper shape, with gaudily dressed actors representing favourite scenes from popular plays, are universal.

Soft balls made of rush pith, wound round with coarse cotton thread, are made to bound from the ground to the palm of the hand, and rebound to keep time to strings of verses, which, however, are little more than repetitions of words. The new year is the time when ball-play is most common.

Battledore and shuttlecock also comes in on the new year. A crowd of boys and girls in a ring, each with a battledore, drive the shuttlecock from one to the other, and a forfeit is paid by whoever misses it—sometimes by a blotch of ink on the face—which does not stain, as with us, it should be remembered, though it smears very readily—or a smart slap with the battledore from the other players on the lower part of the back.

Kishago is a game of filliping shells with the thumb or fore-finger-nail and making cannons. Other games with small shells, beans or pebbles are numerous, and little bags of small beans are thrown into the air from the back of the hand, others are swept up and the descending ones are caught—our game of knuckle-bones, in fact.

Games common to boys and girls are so numerous that a mere enumeration of them would occupy no small space.

Toys of pith, coloured and dried, when put into hot water, tea or *saké*, expand into flowers, groups of flowers or figures. Fans are thrown at targets. There is wrestling with feet, fingers and hands, from the head, ears, teeth and so on;—games of what we call "French and English" &c.

Kite-flying is exclusively a boy's game, though men amuse themselves by helping boys at it. The kites are of various shapes and vary from six inches to as many feet across. The common shape is square, the kite usually bearing some painting on it, mostly a face like an American Indian brave, hideous in war-paint. Some of the smaller kites are like shields, fans, butterflies or figures of men with large sleeves, the larger ones rising to a great height and having 'messengers' or 'travellers' sent up the string. Parachutes are not uncommon.

Folding paper into various curious shapes is mostly a girls' amusement, as is cutting out figures which are painted in colours on sheets.

'Cat's cradle,' puzzles, writing on paper with *saké* and burning it, leaving the design drawn unhurt, or writing with the preparation used for blackening the teeth which when dry is invisible: when the paper is moistened the writing becomes visible again.

Shadows on screens or paper-slides, either with cut figures or with the hands, are common and amusing.

The game known in Europe as *moro*, where one player calls a number, showing at the same time certain fingers, the other player making up the balance, and variations of the game, are common, and is called *Honken*.

Kitsune ken is played by two or three, and then certain positions of the hands represent three things—the two hands held to the ears for the *Kitsune*, or held as if presenting a gun, as the *Teppo* (gun), and held on the hips as the *Danna* (master.) The forfeit is to drink a cup of *saké*. When ready at the call, one, two, three, he who presents the gun at the fox wins; the fox is shot and loses. If the gun is presented at the master the gun loses; gun to gun, fox to fox, master to fox or *vice versâ*. Master to master does not count, and so round goes the game and the *saké* cup, often to the tune of *geyshas'* songs, almost always in their hired companionship.

A similar game is one where the snake, toad and slug are substituted.

Fireworks are of many kinds, rockets, wheels, squibs, crackers and so on, and every autumn sees some new kind produced for the amusement of the boys, and the conversion of their pocket money.

'*Solitaire*,' and a similar game called *Jiu-roku-musashi*, are common.

Drawing lots, writing names on paper and drawing them blindfold, also writing the names of the young girls and young men present and folding them as we do paper-lights, then throwing the bundle down, those falling together being singled out into pairs and the names afterwards read, are common enough. These and such like games afford much amusement to the young folk.

Infants are amused or quieted in many ways by their nurses and frightened into being good by threats of *Onie* (ghosts.)

Hide-and-seek, Blind-man's-buff, &c., are well known.

A boy, with a kerchief over his eyes and his companions round him, throws a tea-cup at one whom he calls by name. Should he hit the one he calls, they change places.

Who stares longest without winking, is a boy's game, and girls surreptitiously try to brazen each other out in the same way. But woe betide them if mamma or nurse catch them and tell papa!

Bamboo stilts are very common among boys in Japan.

Birdlime is much used to catch sparrows, bats, dragon-flies and locusts.

Dragon-flies are caught by tying a female to a switch with fine thread. The male comes and is easily taken.

Mantis-fights are got up by putting two of these insects under a glass.

Pitch-penny is played. Tops, humming, peg and whip, are frequently made of shells and are much in use.

Boys may be seen blowing bubbles through reeds, the water consisting of an infusion of the tobacco stem with alum in it.

Pop-guns, spring-guns, squirts, cross-bows, traps of many kinds, slings, games of racing and jumping, games similar to draughts and chess, of many varieties, are universal.

Toys are very numerous, from cup-and-ball to hobby-horses. Pumpkins are scooped out and a candle is put inside.

Puzzles are very numerous and ingenious; sticks with rings to be taken off, or of thin wood to be put together in some design, may be seen.

Chains of flowers, shells, or pressed flowers, the leaves being pressed between folds of soft paper, leaving their form and colour on the paper, are common.

The list is far from exhausted, but the foregoing is enough to give a fair idea of the amusements and pastimes of the native children.

The third day of the third month is the great annual festival for all girls, great and small, and of all families in which a girl has been born during the previous twelve months. For days previously white *saké*, cakes, cockle-soup &c, are prepared and new robes and girdles are in request. Cherry, Peach, *Keria Japonica*, and some other flowers are used to decorate the house. Formerly figures were made to be launched and sent adrift on a stream on this day. Now, shelves decked with gay covers are set up, on which are laid out dolls and toy sets of furniture, complete marriage *trousseaux* &c. Cakes, tea and food at meal times, are prepared and laid out on miniature table services.

Gosehu, or the 5th day of the 5th month, is the boys' festival, and those who have had a son added to their family during the yearly term make right merry on this occasion. The common people have a large fish of paper, the mouth distended with a hoop, from which it hangs to a long pole. The wind, blowing into the mouth, distends these fish-shaped balloons, and all over the city, as they flaunt gaily, they present a strange sight.

Officers exhibit in front of their houses a stand holding war-banners, lances, &c, and inside the house a room is decked out with toy armour, dolls in fighting costume, representing the ancient heroes, such as Taikō, Yoshitsune, Benke, Tametomo, Asaina &c. Offerings of food are not made, as on the girls' festivals, but a good feast is set out for the boys, at which good wishes are expressed for their success in life and future bravery. The merchants of late years have adopted many of these and other customs formerly practised alone by the *Buké* or officers. The full-grown children and even old men enjoy much of the pastime of the younger people, and have many ways of amusing themselves not open to their offspring before maturity.

Female Accomplishments.

We give these in the order of their importance.

Writing. This is done in the female style of running hand, in the *Hiragana,* and embraces a few Chinese characters. It differs from the classical style, and from that generally used by men, and involves a syntax varying from that of the commonly spoken language, besides containing many expressions and abbreviations not used by men. A special size and quality of paper is used, and the characters employed are large, and curved with an especial gracefulness of form.

Reading is restricted only by the fancy, taste, and talents of the individual, but rarely extends beyond the current literature of the circulating libraries or book-lenders, written in the easiest style, the Chinese characters having the *Hiragana* alongside, to assist the reader in deciphering them. These books are generally love-stories, novels, or accounts of ancient heroes and heroines, dressed up to suit the public taste. Needle-work in this country is unlike that of the fair sex in our own native land, and is little more than what we call tacking, basting, and herring-boning; the cutting out of flounces, skirts, gussets, sleeves, bodices &c., is exceedingly simple, nor do the shapes and fashions change, panniers and crinolines, flounces and trains, being unknown.

Embroidery is the only ornamental needle-work done, and few but tradesmen do much of it. Portions of the underskirts of dresses are frequently embroidered with flowers or simple designs, and the family crest is worked on the upper portion. The elaborately embroidered dresses of the ladies-in-waiting at Court and at the residences of the *daimios* are almost invariably done by tradesmen. Hair-dressing is supposed to be learned, but never acquired to perfection, as it is held to be almost derogatory, and is certainly very difficult.

Cooking is nominally essential to a native lady of accomplishments; indeed, the name of the Shogun's (Tycoon) and great daimios' wives was *Mi-dai-sama* (*mi* honourable; *dai*, kitchen; *sama*, honourable lady). But few are really expert, and men are usually employed as cooks by all above the inferior classes, and at hotels and eating-houses invariably.

Fencing with a short sword, or a halbert with a staff of some four feet in length, was sometimes taught to the daughters of officers, also the throwing of a weapon like a reaping-hook.

Music. The *Koto* (harp), the *samisen* (guitar), especially the latter, is taught to all classes who can afford it, and, of course, to those who are to get their living by it, and perhaps support idle relatives, as is, alas! far too often the case. The *Kokiu, Fuye, Taiko, Tsuzumi* are extra accomplishments rarely found combined in one individual. The national female musical instrument, the *samisen*, has many styles, one of which only is usually taught.* Last, though not least, is the *Odori,* or posturing, learned from the third or fourth to the fourteenth or fifteenth year.

In the provinces girls learn to spin cotton, rear silk-worms, reel off the silk, and weave the thread. Household work is a matter of course, and sometimes manly amusements are learned, such as arranging flowers, *go* (draughts) *shojie* (chess), folding paper into shapes of birds or other objects &c., &c.

---

* The great difference in the styles renders it difficult for the majority of learners to acquire more than one method.

Manly Accomplishments.

Gei Jitzu (Faculty of Accomplishments) may be divided into two great classes.

Bun Gei or Literary; and *Bu Gei* or chivalrous. Eighteen divisions or classes were originally brought over from the Continent (China), but the following is what was taught till the present decade, and is still affected by the conservatives or *Kiu-hei*.

The *Bun Gei* or *Gakumon*, the literature, or rather "Chinese letters" or characters, may be subdivided into *Kan Gaku*, or classics of China; and *Wa Gaku*, or native iterature.

Kan Gaku, or classics of China, and works written in the same style include *Gun Gaku*, or 'War Teachings,' which had several *Riugie* or styles, the principal being *Yamada, Takeda, Togunriu, Echigo, Kurama*, and *Naganuma*.

Ba jitsu (horsemanship) is divided into *Otsubo, Ogasawara, Kisha*.

Jiu jitsu (wrestling) is also taught, but not much practised by gentlemen.

The use of the following weapons is taught:—*Yumi*, archery; it has also its *riugie, Ogasawara* and *Heiki* being the best known.

Kama is a weapon like a bill-hook and is thrown at an enemy. It has its *riugie*, the *Shosetsu, Shinkage* and *Kusare*.

Bo a staff of hard wood a fathom in length, more used by

farmers than by *samurai*. *Nagamaki* is a yard long staff to which a sword is tied, as our rioters would a scythe.

Exercises with the *Tsuku bo satsumata*, the *Mojiri*, and other weapons which were to be seen at the guard-houses in older timses, used to lay hold of dangerous characters, and the methods employed to tie up prisoners with the *Tori nawa*, are also practised.

Shiu-ri-ken was a piece of iron about three inches long, thrown from the hand, a dangerous missile when used by the expert marksman.

Yari (lance) there are many forms of this weapon and styles of using it, such as *Taneda, Hozoin*, &c.

Ken jitzu or Fencing. The principal styles taught are *Shin kage, Shinto, Yagiu, Ono-ha-itto*, and *Ni-to-riu*, or two swords, one for each hand. The *Naginata*, a short lance with a large curved blade, although considered more as a woman's weapon, was taught in the *Shin-kage* and *Shidzuka* systems.

Ho jitsu, or the art of handling fire-arms, has numerous *riugie* or styles, of which the most common are *Inouye, Tatsuke* and *Ogieno*, the latter, introduced with the use of foreign weapons, demands peculiar modes of handling the weapon and is somewhat complicated.

The teachers of fencing, and the use of these weapons after the various styles, most jealously conceal the peculiarities of their methods from all but their pupils, who also are discreet, but the secrets are mainly confined to holding the swords &c., and aiming with the fire-arms.

Under the heading 'weapons' further notice will be taken of details now omitted.

Bun-gei, Polite letters. We will for convenience divide these into *Wa* (native) and *Kan* (classics of China.)

Shin gaku is divided into the *Yoshida kei, Suiega ha,* and formerly there existed some other sects, worshipping at the same shrines, but with somewhat different ceremonies necessary to be studied by the accomplished man.

Wa gaku. The native literature, history and poetry, and the more admired native authors must be known to the Japanese gentleman.

Kan gaku. (Classics.) The standard works of the Chinese classics must be somewhat familiar to assist in composition.

San jitsu. (Arithmetic), is not generally much studied, and many native gentlemen and officers are unable to use the *soraban* (abacus) with facility.

Rei or *Shitzukegata.* Politeness, good behaviour, is absolutely essential, and is studied from the earliest age. The Tokugawas followed the *Ogasawara* style of polite observances. There is also the *Iseriu.*

Shi, consists in composing verses in Chinese.

Outa or native poetry, *renga haikai,* &c., have their admirers. In reciting these verses the voice rises and falls somewhat after the tones of the Chinese. The scholars in the capital may be heard frequently reciting in this, to us, mournful tone.

Taka-Jo, Hawking, was anciently an Imperial pastime: latterly the Tokugawa family and subsequently the great Daimios practised it. It is a sport rarely to be met with now.

Shiukiku or *Kemawari*; Foot ball.   *Yokiu* (small bows).

Fishing, Hunting, Shooting, with the cross-bow, fowling piece or other weapons, boar-spearing, &c., are all more or less affected by the *daimio's* retainers.

The practice of musical instruments also forms part of the accomplishments of a finished gentleman ; he understands too the *No* dances, the arranging of flowers, gardening, &c., and unfortunately many less innocent accomplishments are studied by the young *samurai*. Each had his peculiar hobby, many of them coming under the head of 'Pastimes' or of some special avocation. Men reared in the city or in the provinces had their special and peculiar tastes and experiences, and many of the poorer classes of the *samurai* filled up their time and supplemented their scanty incomes by working at some trade, (*Nai Shoku*.)

Theatres.

Okuni Kabuki, a woman of the province of Idzumo, obtaining the assistance of Nagoya Sansaburo of Owari, thought of collecting money to rebuild the *Oya shiro* of her native province which had been razed during a local disturbance, and about the year of Onin (A.D. 1467) proceeded to Kiôto, and erecting a shed in a place called *Go-jo-kawara*, gave the first public performances, on the grass, hence the name *Shibai*, now commonly called *Shibaya*. There are various other stories told as to the origin and the date of the first theatre or performances. About a century later Onono O-tsu, the maid of Otanounaga, composed a piece on the loves of Joruri Hime, at noted beauty of Sanshiu, and hence comes the name for subsequently composed pieces of the same class, *Joruri*. Chikamatzu Monzaiemon was the next great composer of these pieces, and his compositions are still in favour with the public.

Uji Kadaiyu introduced the *fushi*, the peculiar jerky tones introduced into the readings, so striking to the foreign ear, the exaggeration of which by coolies in the streets at night, sounds as if some one had given the vocalists an unexpected blow. Takemoto Kaku-taiyu and Toyotake Wakataiyu, and Takemoto Gediyu are telebrated as composers of *Gidaiyu*; from the latter came bo called which requires the lower notes and the chest voice, and is more fatiguing.

After the establishment of the rule of the Tokugawas he peaceful state of the country permitted of greate improvements in acting, and players were encouraged in Suruga. Afterwards when Yedo Castle was being built on the site of Ota Dokwan's *Oshiro* (now Nishi Maru), a celebrated actor called Saru-waka Kan-saburo was presented with a 'bâton' *(saihai)* of gold, and sent from Suruga to Yedo in the timber vessels bringing material for the castle. He danced on the piled-up timber and flourished his bâton as the ship came into port.

Since then actors have become popular, and as a consequence numerous; and although they have hitherto been looked upon as a degraded class, of late this disability, in common with those of the *yetas* and others, no longer exists. One family of actors formed an exception to this degraded state, that of Ichikawa Danjuro, now existing in the true line of descent, a rare thing in Japan where adoption is so general. He possessed special qualifications, great ability, and was very accomplished. His descendant at present performs in the principal parts at the new theatre near Shiba, Tokio.

The arrangements of the stage, or *bütai*, are the *mawari-bütai*, or turn table, *seri-dashi* or trap, *seri-agi* or ascent from the stage, and *gundo-gaishi* or topsy-turvey scenes. The passage through the pit by which the actors enter is called *hana-michi* (flower-path.) There are curtains or *makú*, some to drop, others that are rolleded up, and the *ten-makú*, or ceiling-hanging. These are invariably presents from admirers, and inscribed with characters, Chinese and *hiragana*, stating by whom presented, or in case of anonymous gift, *gozonji-yori*, also *shinjo*, (or presented.) Quaint figures are mixed with the characters, and al dyed in various colors, presenting a curious appearance.

The audience is accommodated in the *sajiki*, or boxes, the *udzura* or ground-tier, *taka-doma* or raised pit, *hira-doma* or level pit, and *shiki-fune* or gallery. The latter fronts the stage and is apportioned to the "gods" of the native theatre. There is also the 'official' box. The band, *geza*, is placed on the stage, as also the *gidai-yu* in a stage-box (*chobo*). The prompter is called *kio-gen-sakusha*, and follows the piece with the *MSS.* in hand.

In night performances men with candles fixed on the ends of long sticks hold them so as to throw light upon the actors' faces, in order that the audience may observe their grimaces distinctly. The dressing-rooms consist generally of three stories: the upper for the actors who take the female parts; the second for the superior actors; and the lower, or ground-tier, for the common herd. The principal 'star' is called *Za-gashira,* and the men who come on the stage as horses' legs and such like are called *pê-pê* or *inarimachi.*

Authors, *Kio-gen Saku-sha,* if successful, are looked up to, but the unlucky ones can sometimes find employment only as *hioshigie*—men who rap two pieces of wood on a board at the "points." The *furitsuke* looks after the costumes and general conduct of the piece, scene-shifting &c., the *todori* announces before the rise of the curtain the names &c. of the actors, is in fact a living play-bill. There is a warm bath in the *gaku-ya* (dressing-room), and at each change of character or costume, the actor washes off the paint and cleanses himself preparatory to a new coating.

On the 18th day of the 5th month the actors hold a festival in honour of *Soga,* a piece founded on the revenge of two brothers of that name on their father's murderer, a popular play. It is invariably the opening piece at every theatre at the commencement of the spring season. All respectable playgoers first go to a *chaya* (tea-house) whence they are conducted; seats, refreshment and attendance being guaranteed by the *chaya* people. The "sandwich" of the theatre, called *maku-no-ouchi,* consists of handfuls of rice squeezed, *nigiri-meshi,* and a vegetable stew, *nishime*—as a relish. But although it is not thought correct to bring one's own luncheon, *saké* and any delicacies may be ordered from the cook-shops in the vicinity.

From 6 A.M. to 6 P.M. are the usual hours in order to avoid necessity for artificial light, as in the case of outbreak of fire, the panic would be alarming and accidents numerous. The *Maye Kiogen* is an introduction before the piece commences. Some of the inferior actors, dressed in the ancient court-costume, go through some droll antics, &c. sometimes in the characters of the seven lucky beings *Sichi-fukujin,* &c. or as at *Rai-ko-shi-ten-do-o-jie.*

A portion of a piece, or only the popular portions, or pieces from several plays—an act of each perhaps—may be given on the same day, or a play may stretch over several days. *Yezoshi* are play-bills in book form, and *bantske* the same in sheets. Hand-books of the parts are called *o-mu-seki* (parrot-books, *i.e.* speech without action or feeling).

Females were prohibited to act with men by the Tokugawa government, but there are companies of females who bring out pieces without the aid of men; they do not seem to be popular or numerous, and it is only in a certain class of play that they are at all successful. *To-zai,* East and West, is the "Oyez" of the native theatre; *yerai* or *mai* are the expressions of approbation the audience use when pleased, and sometimes *Nipon-ichi.* There are no "claqueurs," and nothing like our applause or hissing, and there are no *encores* nor calls before the curtain. The approbation of the audience is testified by inviting the popular actor to a feast after the theatre is closed,

Geyshas and *Kakoie-mono* vie in their endeavours to attract the actor's attention, and make him liberal presents.

The popular plays of the Japanese are very numerous: we give a few of their names:—

Soga is a tragedy based on the revenge of two brothers of the murder of their father: the scene is laid in the days of Yoritomo about A.D., 1186.

Chiu-Shin-Gura.—The story of the Forty-seven *Ronins* who in Yedo about 1699 revenged their master's judicial suicide, so well known to all.

Sendai Hagi.—Founded on a story of the attempt to poison the heir of the Sendai Prince, his nurse's devotion and her success by the substitution of her own boy who is poisoned and dies: this is a tale of the early part of the seventeenth century.

Imo Se Yama (The hills of Imo and Sei in Kioto), a story relating the loves of a frail beauty called Hinadori (young-bird) and her sweetheart Koganoske in the beginning of the 16th century.

Kagami Yama.—About the year 1740, in the palace of Matzudaira Simôsá no Kami there was a lady in waiting, a pawnbroker's daughter named *Onoye*. Another of the ladies of the palace named *Iwafuji*, a *samurai's* daughter holding the rank of *Otsubone*, was jealous of the influence and style of *Onoye*, whose father supplied her with ample pocket-money and robes. The latter had amongst her own waiting maids the daughter of a *samurai*, who being heavily indebted to the *Shichi-ya* (pawnshop) begged to have his daughter *Ohatzu* taken into *Onoye's* service. *Iwafuji*, proud of her chivalorus ancestry and her own ability to fence, challenged *Onoye*, whom as a *chonin* (townsman's) daughter she knew to be unpractised in this accomplishment. *Ohatzu* overheard the scoffs and jeers *Iwifuji* poured upon *Onoye*, and being *Iwafuji's* equal by birth, stepped forth as her young mistress's champion and vanquished *Iwafuji* at her own weapons. In the subsequent absence of *Ohatzu*, *Iwafuji's* further insults to *Onoye* ended in the latter committing suicide and *Ohatzu* finally kills *Iwafuji*, and then attempts *gigai* (the female mode of judicial suicide by cutting the throat) but is stopped by the officers of the palace and is finally promoted to *Onoye's* position with the name of "The second *Onoye*," and is rendered happy.

Gem-Pei-Sei-Suie-Ki, the wars of the *Gengi* and *Heiki*. *Taiko-ki*, the wars between the days of the Ashikaga and the Tokugawa, are full of warlike incident, a little illicit love and much murder and rapine. The incidents are taken from the books of the same name, which are standard works.

Ten-jin-ki.—A story about *Tenmangu-Sugawara michizane* who was banished through court intrigue. A woman sacrifices her own child to save his, which was left in charge of one of his former retainers, now a writing-master. Another former servant hears that there is a plot to murder the child and induces his wife to substitute their own child for *Sugawara's*.

Ni-jiu-shi-ko, is a story about *Yaegaki-hime*, who, while her betrothed *Katzuyori* is at the wars, treasures his portrait, and, while gazing on it, sheds tears of grief at his absence, his dangers and the hardships which she is unable to share; and when she hears of his death hangs it up and performs her devotions before it. The fathers of Katzuyori and Yayegaki become enemies, and after many adventures, the former determines to see his betrothed wife, who, he hears, is a great beauty, and enters her father's service as gardener, but is discovered. Eventually by the assistance of foxes he escapes, and they further help the lovers to come together in return for some kindness shewn to the *kitsune* family, but that are never married and Yayegaki soon dies.

Satomi-hak-ken-den.—A famous dog called Yatzubusa was requested by a celebrated warrior to fetch him his enemy's head, and, if obtained, his daughter, the beautiful Fuse-hime, was to be his reward. The dog was successful and brought the head, a great victory being the result. The lady is claimed, she flies to the hills, but, in going to a pool for water, sees herself mirrored on its surface as a dog. Placing her *judzu* (rosary) over her head she recognises her own features; the *judzu* slipping off into the water beyond her reach, she sees again herself reflected as the dog. It seems Fuse-hime had been promised in marriage to a young cavalier before this, and he, in searching for his bride, met the dog Yatzubusa and shot it. Fusehime, although then *enceinte,* committed suicide, and the *fœtus* became a spirit, flying to the eight points, entering eight unborn children, who became brave men. Their adventures are contained in Bakkin's book of the same name as this play.

Inaka Genji is a play adapted from Tanchiko's book of that name. *Mitzu-uji,* a Japanese Adonis or Don Juan, has many adventures and love passages, the ground-work of the piece.

Hiza-kuri-ge, (shanks' mare,) a comic story of a tramp on the Tokaido by Yajirobei and his friend, full of coarse fun, comical incidents and "tricks upon travellers," much of which is quite unfit for translation.

Miaye-no-shinobu, an eldest daughter sold to be an *Oieran* (courtezan). After her father's death, the young sister goes in search of her elder sister, and is entrapped by *zegen* (procureurs); eventually however, the sisters meet and are rescued from their degrading life.

Yao-ya-osichi. Osichi, the green-grocers's daughter, goes to pray at the family temple and sees there her fate, *Kichisa*, with whom she becomes so enamoured that when the gates of the city, dividing the wards, were closed and she could not pass, she, knowing they would be thrown open in case of fire, sounds the alarm-drum, and thereby incurs the penalty of being burnt alive. She is rescued by the discovery that she has been induced to raise the alarm by robbers, who are burned in her stead.

Oshun-Dembei, a piece called after two young lovers who commit suicide locked in each other's embrace, the love portion being tediously spun out to the length of several scenes.

O-han Choyemon.—*O-han*, a girl of fourteen, and *Ohoyemon*, aged forty, love not wisely but too well, and, like the foregoing couple, die together.

Hidaka-juwa. *Kiyohime*, the daughter of a hotel keeper, falls in love with *Anchin*, a priest who periodically stops at the *Yadoya* (hotel). Her importunities frighten the priest, who flees across the river that gives its name to the piece, and hides himself under a temple bell. The girl is, by the power of her love, transformed into a *Ja* (a kind of supernatural serpent), and tracks the object of her desire. Passing round the bell several times it becomes a molten mass by *majinai* (witchery), and consumes both.

Ishikawa Goyemon is a robber of the days of Taiko who is sentenced to be boiled to death in a large pot full of oil.

Kuzu-no-ha, the wife of Abé, when she bears him children, proves to be a fox.

Koku-sen-ya, in 1640, wished to restore the Ming dynasty in China. Kin-sho-jo, his wife, becomes the property of Kanki by capture, and wishing her present master to fight with, and not against, her former lord and master, arranges this by signal—assent being signified by pouring crimson water from her balcony into the stream beneath, dissent by ink-water. She finally succeeds, and the closing scene of the drama shews her on the balcony, pouring out the crimson fluid as a signal of acquiescence.

San-koku-yo-fu-den, is a Chinese novel of tales of three kingdoms, foxes and women, from which incidents are taken and worked up for the stage. *Kiubi-no-kitsune,* the nine-tailed fox is the mischief-maker, taking the form of beautiful women, and disturbing the peace of nations.

It would be as difficult to expunge the Chinese element from Japanese literature as it would be to write about that of Europe without introducing something that had its origin in ancient Rome or Greece. There are no greater literary pirates than the Japanese, who in this respect are even worse than the American re-publishers. The latter sometimes acknowledge the rights of the author which the natives of Japan repudiate. There are other classes of theatres, something between the *hon-shibai*, or true theatre, and the *baba-shibai* or street performers; these are called *yosei*, assemblies principally open at night, most of them similar to the "Penny Gaff" of a seaport-town at home. At these may be seen or heard the *kiogen* of the larger theatres mutilated and murdered, *gidai-yu* and *jorori*, recitations with musical accompaniment, *koshaku*, stories of the wars, *otoshi-banashi* (dropping-down-talk) stories that carry the hearers interest to the sublime, and wind up with a sudden anti-climax.

Tsutsuki-hanashi, continuous talk-stories; *tedzuma*, sleight of hand; *kage*, shadows and rudely-made magic-lanterns, illustrating practical jokes or stories; *hatchi-ningei*, eight-men's parts, one man rapidly changing his character and voice solely sustaining the piece. *Teri-ha-kiogen* is an imitation of *no*. *Chaban* are comicalities, and sometimes "Pepper's ghost" is attempted. *Ayatsuri-niugio* is a puppet show.

Marionettes were first introduced by Haku Taiyu, the *Kannushi* of Nishi-no-miya. *Taiko-ki*, the wars of Taiko in ten acts, is a favorite piece for these puppet-shows. Latterly an additional attraction called *shin-bun*, news, has been introduced by those story-tellers who cater for the poorer class: current events, items from the daily papers, foreign matters, scandal &c., are given, more with regard to the amusement of the audience than to truth or morality.

Baba Shibai (open air performances). The parts are frequently taken by young girls and boys, and *morceaux* of favourite scenes are attempted for the amusement of the crowd, who are expected to throw in a shower of cash at each telling point in the performance.

Pastimes.

Music, studied as a pastime by men, includes the harp. The *Gaku* or Band, composed of several instruments used on Shinto festive or ceremonial occasions, or on official ceremonies of the court, is rarely heard in perfection by the people. The separate instruments are occasionally seen. These we have already described: they are the *sho, sichiriki, taiko, koto, biwa*. Some practise these instruments singly for pleasure, also the *shakuhachi*.

Chess is played in Japan, also *go*, a kind of draughts, deserving a special description, and we merely note them here as the most common games of skill played by both sexes.

In-door pastimes are such as are common to both sexes, though some of them may be but little practised by the gentler half of the nation; yet none of them are exclusively monopolised by men. Indeed, their united participation in these pastimes, here as elsewhere, constitutes at least half their fascination, both at home and in places of public resort. Little beyond a mere enumeration of these games will be attempted now; though, hereafter, a fuller description of the more important of them will be given.

It was not formerly fashionable to have the female

members of an upper-class family exert their musical abilities for the amusement of the head of the house, exhibitions upon the *samisen* being particularly objectionable, as it is the instrument of the common people, and of the less respected classes even of these. On special occasions, however, the daughters were permitted to exhibit their proficiency on the *koto*. This rule has been somewhat relaxed of late, and in addition to the female members of the household, *geyshas (gei-no-aru-mono* or " persons of pleasing accomplishments ") are called in to wait on the guests, but in reality to add life to the entertainment.

Place aux dames:—When the ladies have finished their share of the household duties, which vary in importance with the means of the head of the family and their actual respective positions in the house, have bathed, had their hair dressed, been painted, and have put on their robes and tied their girdles, there is little time left which they cannot wile away over the *hibashi* (charcoal brazier) generally with a tiny pipe and a little tobacco, or their singing or music lessons, if young, for their own benefit, otherwise for that of a young member of the family. Professional needle-women go to each house, so that ladies do little work upon their own clothing, or that of the family. Occasionally a group of young girls may amuse themselves for a while by cutting up scraps of paper and silk which they paste together into pretty shapes, such as flowers, pouches and fancy articles, as presents to their friends, though not to their sweethearts. And here I should remark that the Japanese girl does not have her room and toilet-table covered with those little odds and ends which seem so precious to the European maiden. Some few girls play the native chess, but, as a rule, women in Japan, as elsewhere, love nothing so much as a little gossip or scandal, under the guise of a social chat. If alone, reading a love story is the favourite amusement.

The great resource of men is the game called *go*, played with 180 white discs or counters, cut from the shell of a species of cockle, and 181 black, made from a pebble found near Nachi-no-take (Nachi-waterfall) in Kishiu. The board is divided by lines crossing each other at right angles into 361 squares (19 × 19), the original idea being one square for each day of the year. Each player endeavours to enclose a certain space and prevent his opponent doing the same; they play alternately, laying down one disc at a time. Underneath the *go-ban* or table on which the board is set, there is a square hollow called *chi-tamari* (blood collector). The ancient laws of the game state that if a third person interferes in the play, or tenders his advice or opinion to either party, the intermeddler's head may be chopped off and placed in the hollow of the reversed table which will collect the blood dripping from the severed head. Women often play at *go* together, and sometimes elderly women with men; young men and girls rarely.

Shogi, chess, is common to all sexes and ages, but requires more skill and is much more complicated than any game of this class. The *Shogi-ban* is divided into 81 squares, 9 long and 9 broad—(not 8 × 8 as with us). The *koma*, or chessmen, are, for each player, one *o-sho* king; two *kin-sho*, gold chiefs; two *gin-sho*, silver chiefs;

two *kei-ma,* diagonal moving horse ; two *kio-sha,* perfume-carriages ; one *hisha,* jumping carriage ; one *kaku-gio,* corner-mover ; nine *ho-hei,* foot-soldiers ; in all, twenty, or forty for both sides, which are placed as follows, commencing on the first line of the board next the player, and with the right hand corner: The *kio-sha, kei-ma, gin-sho, kin-sho, o-sho, kin-sho, gin-sho, keima, kio-sha ;* in front of the right hand corner, *kei-ma, shisha;* in front of the left hand corner *kei-ma, kakugio,* and on the third row of squares nine *ho-hei.* The following are the moves of the respective pieces :—

The *o-sho,* one square in any direction.

The *kin-sho,* the same.

The *gin-sho,* one to the front diagonally, to right or left.

Kei-ma to right or left and two forward, hopping over pieces. (Next but one of a different colour ; our knight.)

Kio-sha, straight forward, but not backward, so far as the board is open.

Hi-sha in a straight line in any open direction.

Kaku-gio, diagonal, as far as the board is open.

Ho-hei, one square to the front only.

When any piece has been pushed into the enemy's lines, *i.e.* into those originally occupied by his men, the piece is turned over and becomes a *kin-sho ;* except the the *hi-sha,* which becomes *riu-o* (dragon-king), and *kaku gio* which becomes a *riu-ma,* (dragon horse). Before opening the game the player of the first move is decided by the throwing up of a pawn, as we should a throw up a coin, the other calling *fu* or *kin,* as we should 'head' or 'tail.'

In giving pieces to a weaker player, one *kio-sha* taken off counts one point, two *kio*, two points, one *kaku-sho* three points, and so on. The pieces taken may be placed on any part of the board at the pleasure of the captor, and subsequently played. This game would require a separate chapter to itself in order to describe it fully.

Cha-no-yu. Drinking powdered tea is performed with many ceremonies, which differ for the *usuie* (thin) and the *koie* or thick. The utensils used are few in number, and frequently of great value, not perhaps always intrinsically, but bearing some special worth in the eye of the native *virtuoso*; special invitations are issued to the guests, the usual hour named being noon. The guests assemble in an ante-room, and *o-yu* (hot-water) is presented them in small cups to drink from. They are then escorted into the *cha-dzashkie* (tea-apartment) when the host enters, and, bidding welcome to his guests, prepares to treat them to his tea. Meanwhile certain articles of food are brought in, and the host only attends upon these guests in accordance with minute rules laid down from time immemorial, afterwards the guests withdraw to another apartment leaving the host to complete his preparations. When ready, he strikes a gong and the guests again assemble in the *cha-dzashkie*, and are served with the thick tea in a large bowl from which all drink in turn, each person taking three sips, and passing the bowl to his neighbour. All then retire to the adjoining chamber, where those who smoke are permitted to do so, and the severity of the ceremonial attending the drinking of the *o-cha* is relaxed. The thin tea is then served in cups, one to each guest, and this is replenished as often as may be desired, until the most important person present declares himself satisfied and begs the host to 'forbear,' when the others take the hint, thank the host, and retire with profound mutual compliments. The number of mats (*i.e.* the area) of the apartments and other details are all strictly laid down by minute rules, and here various *riujie* or styles come in, each of which has its advocates. Women and servants are always excluded from this form of entertainment.

Ko-taki, incense burning, is a pastime of a very aristocratic kind, depending chiefly upon the power of recollecting perfumes. There is quite an elaborate set of instruments, or perhaps, rather toys, used, amongst which the principal is a box containing little tickets numbered from one to ten. Several kinds of incense are burned, one after the other, and labelled, after which minute *pastilles* of the same being burnt, each player has to guess the number it bore, depositing a ticket to represent his guess. He who guesses best is first, and so on. This is more a pastime for ladies than for gentlemen, but either may with propriety practice it.

Hana, flowers. *Ike-bana* is the art of arranging flower-vases or holders. The methods and ceremonies are so numerous that a class of men make it their profession, and often in former time made a competence by going from house to house and teaching the art. There are numerous illustrated works on the subject. The chrysanthemum is the *pons asinorum* of learners.

No, native opera, studied by the higher classes, and practised as we do charades or drawing-room theatricals. Masks and gorgeous dresses are used. The pieces, chiefly tragedies, of which there are some two hundred, are based upon stories of the civil wars between the Genji and the Heiki, commonly called *Gempei*, commencing about A. D. 1,150 and continuing at intervals to the end of the century. Between the acts a sort of farce is introduced called *no-kiogen*, which is said to have had its origin in the following story.

A gentleman sent his servant to buy him a fan. The man by mistake bought an umbrella and a series of laughable incidents occur, from the ignorance of the man of his master's dialect. As the whole amusement of the piece depends upon a play on words, it is difficult to understand and impossible to reproduce it. The end, however, is, that the servant dances about with the result of forcing his master to his legs, and and a grand *pas de deux* winds up this comedy of errors, called *Suie-hiro-gari*.

Musical instruments are a source of amusement to many, but few attain any proficiency on them.

Hon-su-roku, is a game played with two dice upon a board divided in half and again sub-divided into eight parts. A black and a white disc, one for each player, is moved according to the number of the dice thrown.

Odori, posturing, is almost exclusively practised by little girls, though 'fast' young men amuse themselves with it when unusually elated.

Painting, writing poetry, making collections of coins, swords, and various other articles, and exhibiting them to friends, are among the numerous modes of passing the dull hours of the well-to-do idle people, such as *daimios* and retired officers. Exceptional hobbies, collecting birds or animals, botany, horticulture &c., are sometimes turned to profitable account now that the revenues of idle people have been diminished. Horsemanship takes the first place, although it is only a few years since the higher classes alone were permitted to ride in public. Of games on horseback, *dakiu*, or ball-throwing, is played with small balls like those used in racket-courts, which are picked up off the ground with a stick on the end of which there is a small loop or net, and thrown through a hole in boarding at the end of the course. The players are divided into sides, for instance, the *Gem* and the *Pei*, and a certain number of balls is decided upon. The side which succeeds in holeing the greatest number of balls of course wins.

Kisha is archery on horseback, with a small target at one end of the course.

Tori Awase, was formerly practised at Kioto by the *kugés* (nobles), but, being prohibited, it is now not much seen.

Shamo, Cochin China fowls are secretly matched in fight. This is also called *keai* (met-to-kick). Exhibitions of birds, flowers, plants &c. are numerous and common.

Pic-nics and mushroom-gatherings, pleasure parties in the holidays to the shrines, temples or gardens, the special occasions of the blossoming of the plum, cherry, *s hobu* (Acoruo Calamus) and chrysanthemum, or the special festivals of the more noted places of pilgrimage, are amongst the amusements of the year. Cockle-gathering is eminently the sport of girls and children, as is also herb-gathering,

Fishing with rod and line, or spearing, fishing with casting nets and trawling, are favourite sports with men of all classes.

Shiu-kiku is an aristocratic game not much practised now. Archery has also been little practised of late. There are other sports of which we shall treat, but they will fall under a different heading.

Young men often have amusements not always of a kind to bear description in this place, the mildest form of these taking the shape of "sprees" or entertainments with their friends, plenty of *saké* and the company of singing and dancing girls the leading features.

Besides the manlier sports and accomplishments described elsewhere there is the usual round of dawdling pastimes for hours hanging dull and heavy; some of these we note to give an idea of their general character. Many are only known to the officers, and the retired and old official, daimio, and wealthy trader devote much time to the study of one and all.

Music Teachers.

Shisho, or Teachers of Music in its higher branches, are generally men; but female teachers, though not considered such perfect musicians, are more commonly employed as instructors to girls and young women. If greater proficiency is subsequently desired, a male teacher is employed. The *koto* is most frequently taught by blind men. Teachers who devote themselves to other instruments than the *koto* and the *samisen* are very rarely met with in every-day life. *Geyshas*, who are noted as good musicians, when they become elderly and less attractive to guests, frequently marry, and adopt the profession of teachers of the *samisen*. Each instructor devotes himself exclusively to one of the hereafter-mentioned styles, and although some pupils attempt several *riugie*, little, if any, progress is made under these circumstances, the teachers being opposed to the blending of different styles, while the difference between the methods of playing and of toning the voice, cause confusion.

With young children the teacher is obliged to hold the pupil's hands and place the fingers for each note, and when some progress has been made the pupil and teacher squat down *vis-à-vis*, the pupil watching the teacher's fingers and endeavouring to imitate each movement of them until a simple tune is learned. No scale or ideas of musical notation are attempted; the lesson is learned by simple imitation and memory. Some books have been printed to facilitate music teaching and self-instruction, but they are scarce and rarely used, and do little more than shew the position of the fingers on the finger-board. Sometimes the teacher plays the accompaniment while the pupil sings.

Samisen-playing alone is rarely taught, singing and recitation with *samisen* accompaniment being much more usual. Those pupils who desire to become teachers receive a name from their teacher after having attained a certain proficiency; without this they cannot teach publicly, being without musical reputation.

With the exception of *Naga-outa*, all singing and recitation with *samisen* accompaniments, is called *Joruri*, after Joruri Hime,* whose loves and sorrows are said to have formed the subjects of the first compositions of which Otsu is the reputed author *(Vide Section* Theatres*).*

Gidai-yu-buschi: In 1575 lived Takemoto Gidaiyu, who was the originator of this style, and his music is written for male voices in the lower tones. The *samisen* used is of the largest size, the strings are thicker, and the *batchi* is heavier than customary, and the playing *staccato.* The subjects are usually tragic and warlike, and more frequently draw tears from the audience than any other class of music. It forms the ordinary accompaniment to the native stage, and is mixed up with the actors' parts, joining broken links in the dialague, or explaining the soliloquies, motives of the characters, &c. which the words and action of the players may fail to convey.

Tokiwazu. Komoji daiyu introduced this style at the beginning of the present century, and it is now very common among children. The falsetto is cultivated for this style, and the subjects of the songs are love-stories, nor is it in any way strange to hear innocent little girls straining their voices to the highest pitch, unconsciously

---

* Joruri Homi, whose love adventures are related by Otsu, and considered as the first of the now innumerable imitations and variations. She was a native of Yahagi-no-hashi of Sanshiu, the daughter of Kiichi. Her lover was Ushi waka maru, who afterwards became Yoshitsune, brother of Yoritomo, A.D. 1177 (about).

Ushi waka was fond of flute playing, and very clever. One moonlight night he wandered, playing his flute; when he approached a house where some one was playing the koto. Presently the player changed the tune to match the flute, to the mutual delight of both; there was a meeting between the unconscious and unknown duet players, and mutual love at first sight. The sequel is a long life of fruitless love, that forms an inexhaustible fund for the story-tellers.

reciting the most indecent love passages, stories of runaway matches, the joint suicide of lovers &c. The strings of the *samisen* used are of medium size, and the accompaniment to the *Tokiwazu* songs is called *kishi-sawa*.

Kiyomoto, was brought out by Yenjiu-daiyu, also early in the present century. The head-voice is cultivated for this music, and the subjects of the songs are mostly love-stories, more lively and amusing as well as comparatively more decent than the *Tokiwazu*. This style is very popular with young girls, and is the style generally learned by the *geyshas*. The *samisen* used is of medium size.

Tomimoto. This style was introduced about fifty years ago by a teacher named Bungo, and somewhat resembles the *Giduiyu* style, softened down, interspersed with love-stories, of a more sober character than the *Tokiwazu* style. The chest-voice is chiefly employed, the middle voice occasionally, the *falsetto* rarely, and a medium-sized instrument is used. The accompaniments are called *Sasaki*.

Kishisawa was originally the accompaniment to the *Tokiwazu* singing; but about 1860 the teachers quarrelled and were brought before the magistrates, who, being unable to decide who was most to blame, permitted a division and the establishment of a new style. There is little difference between *Kishisawa* and *Tokiwazu* worth noting here, and but slight regard is paid to it now-a-days.

Kato, (East River); called after the music teacher who introduced this style. The stories are mostly founded upon heroic actions and celebrated occurrences mixed up with a few love-stories. The natural voice is used. The

Samisen used is of a special size and form, smaller than the medium size. This style is not much taught at present. It has always been fashionable and is patronized by amateurs exclusively. A play called Otokodate-no-Skeroku requires a *kato* accompaniment, when amateurs must be obtained. They play with masks on, and, as they do not take payment, are entertained in return with feasting and fun. This is the only instance of amateur performances in theatres.

Ichi-chiyu-bushi was introduced by Ichi-chiu, a teacher, some sixty years ago, and resembles the *kato*, but is more plebeian in style and more entertaining. Although most of the scenes are laid in the Yedo *yoshi-wara*, yet, as a rule, they are tolerably decent. Each song has some quaint name, These are of two classes, *miako* and *uji*. There is a special form of *samisen* of medium size for these songs.

Naga-outa was improved and brought into notice by Kineya Rokuzaimon early in this century. It consisted originally mostly of accompaniments alone, but songs were composed to suit them. These songs are called *Uta-utai.* There are various styles in singing, called *Yoshimura, Matzunaga, Fujita* and *Okayasu,* in which the highest notes of the falsetto predominate. The burden of the songs is generally decent. One of them called *Oie-matsu* (old pine-tree) runs literally thus.

   Shin-no-shi-ko
   Mikari no toki
   Ten niwakani kaki kumori
   Tai yu shikirini furi shikaba
   Mikado ame wo shinogan to.

Ko matsu no kage ni
Tatchi yoreba
Kono matsu tatchi machi
Tai boku to nari
Yeda wo tare ha wo kasane

Kono ame wo morasa zari shikaba Mikado
Tai yu to iu shaku wo
Kono matszu ni okuri
Tamaishi yori
Matsu-wo Tai yu to mousu to kaya.

TRANSLATION.

Shin-no-shi-kô
Once a hawking did go;
But the clouds they lowered
And down the rain poured
   Ho! the Emperor must not get wet.

That old pine tree
Good shelter will be,
And under it he did go;
When the branches bent so
   Through the leaves the rain could not get.

The Emperor's whim
Was to have the tree giv'n
A *Shaku* with *Tai-yu* writ thereon,
And immediately thus it was done,
   For the pine tree's named *Tai-yu* e'en yet.

The *samisen* used is the smallest, the *sawa* the thinnest, the strings the finest, and the *batchi* the lightest. This is the most difficult style to acquire perfectly, and is taught to all young ladies of good family. Whatever style may afterwards be taught, the gentry always desire that their children should begin with this.

Shinnai, introduced by Tsuruga Shinnai, fifty years ago, comprises songs about courtesans and their patrons. At night men and women may be met with, their faces concealed by the rag of the towel which answers so many purposes, twanging their *samisens*. Those who wish to hear them sing, call them, but do not admit them into their houses. A favourite piece is called *Akegarasu*—the story of a courtesan Urazato and her guest, Tokijiro, of whom she became very fond, so that when all his money was spent she still enticed him to visit her. Her master finding this out, put Tokijiro into a cask, tied up the girl and beat her; Finally, they escape together. There are two styles; the *Okamoto* is considered respectable, but the *Fujimatsu* is very coarse and indecent. The *samisen* used is small; the voice falsetto with a nasal twang. Children are not often taught the *shinnai*.

Hayari outa. Outazawa Nourokusai, during the last generation, was the first and great composer of this variety of music, consisting chiefly of short verses. The *geyshas* entertain their patrons with this class of singing, and often improvise their own verses for the occasion. The words and accompaniment to the *Odori* are usually *Hayari-outa*. Teachers of *geyshas* study this style of composition. Respectable families prohibit it.

Japanese Cosmogony.

Konton, chaos, like an egg or embryo, was the normal condition of all things before the separation, according to the Chinese philosophy, of the two 'principles,' *in*, the female, and *yo*, the male. The ethereal ascended and became the heavens, the sediment was precipitated, from which the *ashi* (Ereyanthus japonica) sprang up like a young shoot. This shoot grew until it became the first of the *kami*, now called Kuni-toko-tachi-no mikoto (the first being of the country) followed by the appearance of Kuni sazu chi no mikoto (the being who pushed his way into a circumscribed space), and Toyokunnu no mikoto (the being who made the land pleasant and lively), who represents the first fruits of the earth after chaos. Then successively appeared the following:—

Takami-musubi-no-mikoto (offspring of heaven and earth.)

Kami musubi no mikoto, (offspring of the gods.)

Uji hi ni no mikoto (offspring of the ground.)

Ama no toko tatchi no mikoto (offspring of the heavens.)

Kuni no soko tatchi no mikoto (the kami like unto kumi toko tatchi.

Toyukumuno kami (God of plentiful vegetation.)

Uhi chi ni no kami (God of the earth).

Sui chi ni no kami (God of sand).

Sahi no kami (God of useful timber).

Kahi no kami (God of unfelled timber).

Oto no chi no kami (God of harvests).

Oto no be no kami (God of husbandry).

Omotaru no kami (God of primeval habitations).

Aya kashi ko ne no kami (God of primitive dwelling places).

Up to this period the male principle *yo* being paramount, the sexes had not appeared. The foregoing represent the creation.

The five elements, wood, fire, metal, earth, water, were

now divided, and in due order fulfilled their respective uses. Isanagi, the produce of the male, and Isanami that of the female, come next, and these constitute the first couple. The names are derived from the meaning of the first words spoken upon earth, the woman beckoned to the man, he nodding assent and going. They stood on the celestial bridge which spans the ethereal vault (amano uki hachi), the man waving the *Tama boko* (matchless falchion). The thought arose that there may be substance beneath the face of the unstable waters, and he plunged the mighty weapon into the watery depths, and the drops which trickled from it when withdrawn formed the dry land, called *Onokoro shima* (the inconsiderable island). To this they both betook themselves, designing to make it the pillar of a future continent, and started to make the circuit of it, the woman turning to the right, the man to the left. They met at the other side, when the woman spoke the first words uttered upon earth, *Ana niyashi mashi otoko ni ainu* (Oh joy to meet a lovely man!) But the man was displeased that the woman spoke first and insisted that the journey round the island should be repeated, and when they again met, the man said *Ana niyashi mashi ootome ni ainu,* (Oh joy to meet a lovely woman!) Thus was the creation of man perfected, and the island grew into Oyamato toyoakitsusu, (the everlasting great Nipon.)

The woman Isanami conceived and brought forth a female child, either as a punishment for having spoken before the man, or because the female principle, *in*, was more powerful. The man was greatly disappointed that a son was not born.

This female child became Tenshoko dai jin. Isanami brought forth a second female child called Tsuki yomi no mikoto, (the goddess of moon—the moon itself), and again a third child, a male, named Hiro ko (leech). At the age of three, being still unable to walk, his parents made for him a boat of *kusunoki* (camphor-tree) in which he was sent adrift, and he became the first fisherman. He is called Yebisu, and is worshipped yearly by fishermen and by traders—catching fish and selling them being considered the first commercial transaction.

A fourth child was born to them, Sosa no no mikoto, a goodly-shaped boy, who was doubly welcome after the former female children and the cripple, and their hopes rested on their last-born to populate the country. But they were fated to disappointment as the boy proved most unruly, and the older he grew the more intractable he became, murdering his countrymen, and tearing up trees and destroying vegetation. His parents were therefore compelled to condemn him to banishment and decided to send him to a distant land *Ne no kuni*, whither he went. He returned, however, and continued his wild career, on one occasion turning a wild horse loose into the field his sister Tenshoko had planted with rice; the plants were trampled down and the fields destroyed. Again, after she had erected a dwelling in which to prepare the new rice for her food, he defiled it so that it could no longer be used; and on another occasion, when she was sitting at her loom weaving, he threw a rocking horse's hide violently upon it, and prevented her working further. This repeated misconduct became to her so unbearable that she took refuge in *Ama no iwato,* the celestial cavern, and drew a huge rock to the mouth of the cave to close herself in. *Rikugo,* i. e. *Ten Chi Shi-ho,* heaven, earth and the four quarters, became enveloped in darkness, and there was no distinction between day and night, and the *Yaso yorozu no kami,* eight hundred thousand gods, assembled at *Amano yasu no kawara* (the heavenly riverplain of Yasu), to discuss what was to be done to restore light to the world, and procured from Tokoyo, the country of perpetual day, a number of *naga naki niwa tori* (continuously crowing domestic fowl) which were plentiful there. These irrepressible chanticleers were brought before the mouth of the cave, and Tatchi kara-o-no-kami, the strong-handed god, stood there waiting. From Ama-no-kaku yama, Futodamano mikoto (exceeding beauteous god) uprooted and brought a large tree of the kind called *Sakaki,* from the top branch of which were hung five hundred jewels *(tama)*; from the centre branch was suspended a *yadi no kagame* (a starshaped mirror), and from the lower branch were hung green and white slips of paper *(nigite)* and this tree was also brought to the entrance of the cave. The gods now implored Tenshoko to show her face, but she was deaf to their entreaties. Then Ama no usume no mikoto (the heavenly glossy-countenanced goddess), advised their dancing before the cave to excite the curiosity of the self-imprisoned goddess, and she took the branches of the tree brought by Futodama, and decking her hair with the ornaments suspended from it, she took a bamboo, to the end of which some *chikaya* (a grass) was tied, to look like a spear, tying up her long flowing sleeves with tendrils of ivy. These preparations completed, bonfires were lighted, and Ama no usume danced before the cave with all her might, to the music of fifes, drums and cymbals. Tenshoko, hearing the music and dancing, wondered what it was that could cause such joy since Toyo ashiwara had become *Tokoyami* (darkness) by her entering the cave, and that there was therefore more cause for grief than joy; thus her curiosity led her to move the great rock slightly to peep out on the ill-timed scene. Tatchi-kara immediately seized the stone and drew it away, and grasping her hand drew out Tenshoku, when Waka tomi-no-kami and Imbei no kami (the god of shades), made a rope of rice-straw, which they twisted the contrary way, from left to right, and which they drew across the mouth of the cave. Then all was gladness, and the rotation of day and night was established again for evermore. As a punishment to Sosano, the cause of all this trouble, instead of death, his hair was pulled out hair by hair, his finger and toe-nails extracted, and he was again banished to a far distant land. This story contains the first accounts of music, where the gods play to the dancing. It is the original from which the Kagura (dancing and music before the *miyas*) was copied. It is also the first instance of a female receiving anything from the hands of a man to adorn her person, and this was used to place in her hair—hence the first hair-pins. We also have the first allusion to back-handed straw-rope (*shiri-kume-nawa*, a rope to prevent return) being used, and although with some modifications, the origin of straw-rope round trees, shrines, houses &c., often seen at new-year time and at Shintô festivals. The *taske* (sleeve-binder) is also first mentioned, although then ivy-tendrils. The adornment of the branches of the tree finds its counterpart to this day in the *magatama* (waving jewels), small willow trees with numerous trinkets suspended from them.

Isanami brought forth a fifth child, a male, called Hino-kamikaku tsuchi (god of wild-fire) and on that day she was consumed by fire. In the agonies of death she brought forth Tsutchi no kami hani yama hime (the goddess of the earth and hills) also Midzuhanome no kami (goddess of water). Kaku tsuchi took Hani yama to wife, and in due time she bore him Wakamusubi, the first produce of man and earth, on whose head grew the mulberry and silk-worm, and from whose navel sprung the five cereals (*go koku*), rice, wheat, beans, millet and sorghum, the *Sundamono*, or purer principle, rising to the upper extremity as the silk-worm; the *Nigoru mono* (sediment) sinking into the produce of the ground. There are many versions of these accounts, differing somewhat in detail, and some of them have been translated and printed in Europe long ago.

Isanami's tomb is in Arima no mura, in the province of Kishiu, and when the blossoms appear on the trees flowers are taken to the tomb. Isanagi, finding the country he had created subject to thick fogs, wished to dispel them, and dispersed them with the force of his lungs, his breath becoming Shina tobe no kami (the god by the sea). Because his partner was consumed by the fire of Kaku tsuchi,

Isanagi cut him into three portions; the upper portion became Ika tsuchi no kami (the God drummer, the god of thunder); the centre portion O yama tsumi no kami (god of abundant water); and Taka wo.kami (the god of storms). Isanagi then ordered that his children should divide their duties properly between them. Tensho should control Takamanohara; Tskiyomi should assist Tenshoko; and Sosanono should control Awo una bara (the plains of green sea, by which is meant the world.) Tenshoko then enquired for the god of food and sent Tokiyomi for him. He appeared, and facing the land, breathed and his breath became *Ii* (boiled rice). He then faced the sea and breathed and his breath became fish, broad and narrow. Then, facing the hills he breathed again, and beasts with coarse hair appeared (boar, deer &c.) and beasts with fine hair (rabbits &c.). Collecting some of these he placed them before Tski yomi, who was enraged at being presented with what had come from the mouth of the god of food, and slew him, and reported this to Tenshoko who degraded Tskiyomi from joint rule and condemned her to appear only by night while Tensho slept. Ama no kuma hito was sent to see what had become of the slaughtered god, and found him dead, but his head had become horses and oxen; from his forehead grew millet; from his eyebrows crawled silk worms; from his eyes sorghum; from his bosom sprang rice; from his loins, wheat and beans. These were taken and presented to Tenshoko and she apportioned them as human food.

Religion.

The two principal religions of this country are Shintoism and Buddhism; and, besides these, Confucianism has been rapidly gaining ground of late years.

Shintoism—from *Shin* (gods) and *To* (road) or *Kami no michi,* deserves the first place as the ancient *cultus* of the country. Little more than a bare outline of it can be sketched here, though some interesting matter connected with it will appear subsequently.

The Shinto idea of creation is that out of choas (*konton*) the earth *(in)* was the sediment precipitated, and the Heavens (*yo*) the ethereal essences which ascended; man (*jin*) appeared between the two. The first man was called Kuni-toko tatchi-no-mikoto, but five other names were given to him, and then the human race appeared, male and female. Isanagi and Isanami begat Tenshoko daijin, the first of the five gods of the earth.

Jimmu tenno, the son of Fukiawasezu no mikoto, was the first Mikado (B. C. 660) and from the date of his accession the Japanese *ki gen* commences, 2,535 years ago. The present Mikado, Mutzhito, is the 123rd of the line.

The *Kami,* with one exception, are historical personages who have been deified, and petitions are offered to them, as will be presently explained, although in the prayers offered up at the Shinto shrines called *Miya, Gu, Yashiro* or *Jinsha,* there is nothing indicative of a belief in a future state, or of the possession of a soul by the petitioner.

Formerly the priests of the Buddhist creed amalgamated their doctrines with the petitions of the Shinto faith, and supplied this deficiency, but the scepticism of the men of the day induced them to taken advantage of the low state of morality among the Buddhist priests to bring about a separation of the two systems of worship and belief, and Shintoism is once more the established religion of Japan.

The Japanese *Kami* (gods) number 13,730, of which about 3,700 are known to have shrines; to the more celebrated of these shrines have been erected throughout the Empire; those to Inari, for instance, may be found in every town and district and in every land-owner's residence, noble and peasant.

Each province has its *Ichi-no-miya*, and each district, sometimes each hamlet, may have one or more local *Kami*.

The petitions offered up at the *Miya* (shrine) are called *Roku-kon-no-harai* (petitions of six origins), Anger, Grief, Kindness, Protection, Dishonesty and Avarice or Selfishness.

Sai-mon, or thanksgivings for favours granted, or successes attained, are offered up.

Notto, or songs of praise are used by the *Kan-nushi*, or guardian of the *Miya*.

Each *Kami* has an annual festival, and many have particular days in each month, on which it is usual to visit the *miya*, besides which petitioners visit the shrines at all times, but rarely after sundown. The ceremonies and observances are most minute and vary for each *Kami*. We subjoin one of the more common prayers offered up by the devotees at the *Miya*. Generally, however, the hands are clapped twice and the genuflexions are made in silence. Both sexes may use the *harai* or prayers. Books are not generally used, nor are prayers learned by rote for the occasion. The *Kami* is supposed to read the prayer while yet but in thought, and before it rises to the lips in the form of words. Not being intended for human ears, eloquence is not needed. Females are rarely to be seen praying at Shinto shrines.

(*A prayer of the first importance.*)

God that in the high celestial plains exists! gracious monarch! godlike in substance and godlike in intellect! heavenly words of praise are offered up: therefore give protection from guilt and its punishments, banish such and purify uncleanness. Host of Gods! give ear and listen to these our petitions.

SAI YO NO HARAI.

(*Taka ma no hara ni kami todomari-mashi-masu, Sume mutzu, kami rogi kami romi no mikoto, wo motte, Hona tsu notto no Futo notto no koto, noré-kaku, noraba tsumi to iu tsumi toga to iu toga wa araji mono wo to harai tamaye kiyome tamafu to mousu, koto no yoshi wo moro moro no kami tatchi, sawo shika no yatzu no on mimi wo furi tatete kiko shimese to mousu.*)

The world is often called in poetry, *Toyoashi nara* (the fruitful rush-plain) from the *Ashi* (*Eryanthus Japonicus*) the first-fruit of the earth after chaos.

Takama-no-hara are the high plains of heaven, where the gods dwell, but from which mortals are excluded,

Drums (*taiko*) are beaten on festive occasions, and at some temples the devotee calls the attention of the *kami* by shaking the *suzu*, a thin metal globe suspended above him containing several pellets which rattle when so shaken by the long tassel which is fastened to it for the purpose. All *miya* have a mirror on the altar, as an emblem of purity; therefore it is said that the word *kami* is a modern name for the gods represented by the Chinese character *shin*, and is derived from *kagami*, a mirror, omitting the repetition of the first syllable.

All *Miya* have one or more *Tori-i* (bird-perches), which are usually offerings by devotees or petitioners as thank erections. He who approaches the *Miya* must pass under the *Tori-i*, and then the *Hai-den* or place of prayer, is reached, at the rear of which is another building, the *Hon sha*, or true *Miya*. With few variations the same style of architicture prevails throughout the Empire. Sometimes a gateway with a porch on each side is to be seen, and in each porch a figure seated or mounted, called the guardian of the right and the left, * called *Yuki* and *Suki*.

The *Go-hei*, made of paper cut in a peculiar form, inserted in the split end of a piece of bamboo, is an emblem of purity, and is enclosed in a box, thus forming the *Shintai* which is placed in the innermost shrine.

To be *fujio*, unclean, precludes worship at the *Miya*; on the death of a parent for fifty days; of a child, twenty;

---

* Columbus' Account of the Cemies, and the worship of ancestors in the islands of the West Indies bear a striking resemblance to the forms of the *Kami* worship.

women after child-birth, twenty-one days, &c.; eating flesh or shedding blood, until the next day; at the expiration of these periods, bathing and change of raiment are requisite.

The *Kannushi*, keeper of the *Miya*, also called *Shinshoku* (or *Shinkan* in correspondence) was an hereditary position, but of late the *Kiobusho* (Department of Religion) examine candidates. The subordinate positions vary in duties and titles with each *Miya*, men only being employed to read the *Notto* and keep the *Miya* in order.

The *Kagura* is the music and dancing on the annual, monthly and other special days, offered up to the gods, but intended also to amuse the visitors at the *Miya*. The *Taiko* (large drum), *Fakko* (small drum,) and *Fuye* (flute) form "the band," while performers with special dresses and masks go through various antics in silence. There is no design, and no set pieces, merely changes of dress. Some of the characters represented are predecessors of Jimmu fighting with evil spirits and defeating them; but a little comicality is introduced, practical jokes are travestied and the fox is not forgotten—the fox and the monkey have a trial of wit, and so on. This is generally preceded by the appearance of the *Miko* (child of the gods), a female dressed in white, with a necklace of flax, bearing a *Gohei* in her right hand, and jingling in the left a *susu* of peculiar shape. This is the only part taken by females in the Shintô rites.

The offerings, *Sonaye-mono*, are *Miki* or *Onsake* in two vases with paper inserted in them; *Arai-yone* cleaned rice in unglazed pottery; *Mochi*, cakes of boiled and pounded rice; and, on special occasions, *Kowa meshi* or *seki-han*, rice boiled with *Adzuki*, small red beans. Fruit and vegetables of all kinds in season; fish, generally the *Tai*, (*Serranus Marginalus,*) which are not allowed to spoil, but converted to the use of the *Kannushi*, the *Shisho* or inferior officials and others connected with the *Miya*.

The following are the most important *Kami*, and the salient points in the adoration of each is merely noted.

Ten-sho-ko-dai-jin or *Ama-terasu-no-kami*, is the first and principal of the *Kami* and the only one of whom there is no historical record of life on this earth. This goddess is highly venerated as the ancestor of Jimmu, and therefore of the present Imperial family. The principal *miya* are in Isé, called *Dai-jin Gu*, where there are two, the older, called the "outer," the other, the 'inner.' There are shrines throughout the Empire, but there is no regular distribution of them, all depending on the local popular fancy. When a deputation of the subscribers to the proposed building undertake a pilgrimage to Isé and return with the *Shintai* (godly substance) consisting of a small box of paper on a wooden framework, containing paper cut and stuck on a slip of bamboo; on the box is written five Chinese characters meaning "Waved respectfully ten thousand times," equivalent to so many prayers. This is placed in the Holy of Holies concealed from vulgar gaze. Formerly every household procured a *Shintai* every new year from Isé, now the Kiobusho distributes them when necessary, but not annually.

In Isé there is no annual festival, but the number of pilgrims is greatest in the Spring. At the other *Miya* annual *Matzuri* (festivals) are fixed according to local convenience.

The pilgrimage to Isé is the most general; all devout men and women are supposed to go at least once, and pilgrims from the remotest corners of the Empire resort thither and receive the *Shintai* to take home. Poor people are frequently met begging their way thither, but they are not expected to wear any peculiar garb.

Sumi yoshi is the name of a celebrated *Miya* near Osaka, erected in honour of Jin-gu-ko-go who was the 15th Mikado A.D. 200 to 268, and who is the patron *kami* of all who go on the water either as sailors or travellers.

Soko-tsutsu-no-mikoto (God of the bottom of the Sea), *Naka tsutsu-no-mikoto* (God of the middle of the Sea), and *Uwa-tsutu-no-mikoto* (God of the surface and controller of the waves), three *kami* who are placed after the time of Kuni toko and before Jimmu, and the Gods of the Sea are incorporated with Jin-gu, and called *Sumi-yoshi-shi-sha* (fortunate residence of the four incorporated *Kami*).

Guion, Go-dzu-tenno, Suga jin sha (Ox, Chief, heavenly king) or Sosa no-ono-no-mikoto is the *Kami* of the cavaliers: the shrines are to be met with in all provinces, the principal one being in Kioto. The great annual festival is on the 15th day of the 6th month, and was one of the principal festivals of Kioto. There are several shrines in Yedo, but the date of the principal festival differs there.

Inari, or, more correctly, *Uga-no mitama no kami*, is the God of the produce of the soil, cereals, vetetables, &c., commonly called *Inari* (rice-stalk bearer) and the shrines may be recognized by the *Tori-i* or portal being coloured red with carved stone foxes on either side. Besides the larger shrines met with at almost every turn, each landholder or farmer has one on his property.

The *Kitsune*, (fox), frequently seen at the shrines, attracted thither by the offerings of food, became gradually associated with Inari. The annual festival is on the first day of the horse, which occurs in the second month.

Hachiman or *Ojin Tenno*, the 16th Mikado, who reigned from A.D. 270 to 309, is the God of Warriors. He was buried at Usa in the province of Buzen where the chief shrine is, and there is no province, county *(korie)* or town without one or more dedicated to Hachiman. The annual festival is held on the 15th day of the 8th month.

Tate minakăta no mikoto is the name of a God whose principal shrine is at Suwa in Shinshiu. On the festivals, a deer's head is placed before the shrine as an offering. Hitherto, the Japanese, who had a great dread of eating flesh, used to obtain a pair of the chop-sticks which are sold at this shrine, and with which they may eat flesh without evil befalling them.

To-sho-gu is Gongen* or Iyeyasu, the first Tokugawa Shogun, who obtained this rank in 1603, and abdicated after three years in favour of his son Hidetada, himself becoming Ogoshosama. He died in 1616, and was first buried at Kunosan in Suruga, but was afterwards removed and buried in Nikko in the province of Shimotské. There are shrines throughout the Empire dedicated to

---

* There are many other *Gongen* : it is a posthumous title of the Buddhist Saints.

him. The 17th day of the 4th month is the date of his chief festival, but his shrine is also visited on the 17th day of each month.

Ten-jin, or *Ten man gu*, Suga-wara-no michi-sane, who was Saki no Udaijin to Daigo tenno, the 89th Mikado. He was banished to the province of Chikuzen and there died in 903, and was buried in a place called Dai-sai-fu, where a shrine to him was afterwards erected, Others have since sprung up throughout these islands, where he is prayed to as the patron saint of learning, and, of course, of scholars and students. The 28th day of the 5th month is his great festival or *Matsouri*. In Yedo, *Kame-ido* is his principal shrine.

The accounts of Shintoism which have been published hitherto, from the days of Xavier's successors to the present time, contain much of the Buddhist rites, which had been engrafted upon the old faith. The latest important object of deification or canonization was Gongen, called Toshogu, who received the honour A.D. 1627.

The *Chokkio*, like a papal Bull, always emanated from Kioto (*i.e.* the Mikado.)

On the thirtieth day after the birth of a male, and thirty first after the birth of a female child, it is taken to the *Miya* of the district and, according to the means of the parent, so many *Harai* are repeated, and the *Gohei* is waved before the shrine. There is no baptism or similar ceremony. The *Kami* of the *Miya* to which the child is taken is called *Ubusuna** (god of the place of birth) and

---

* *Uji-gami*, is frequently confounded with the *Ubusuna*. The former is the family ancestral patron; the latter the local *kami* of the place of birth.

becomes the patron *Kami* of the child, who has received its name on the seventh day after birth from one chosen by his parents with the advice of friends or the priests. Thenceforth female children on the 15th of the 11th month of their third year, when the hair is allowed to grow, on their seventh year, the *Obitoki*, time to wear the broad girdle, and thirteenth year, the earliest age to dye the teeth visit the *Miya*.

Male children, on the same day of the month, in their fifth year when first 'breeched' with the *Hakama*, and usually when the head if first dressed after the manner of adults are taken to the Ubusuna *Miya*.

Formerly *Junshi* (to accompany the dead) was practised by the upper classes. When the master died his wife and most faithful retainers prepared to accompany him and committed suicide. Later on, about the beginning of our era, Haji no tsukune, the ancestor of Suga-wara-no michi-sane, made figures of clay to substitute for those who intended to immolate themselves. Although the rite was prohibited, it was still at times practised in defiance of the law.† Penances, charity or alms-giving, self-imposed pain, fasting and mortification of the flesh and spirit are not required by the *Kami*, but men must lead a pure life, be honest, truthful and chaste.

Good works consist in repairing or improving the *Miya*, but a number of Buddhist ideas are intermingled by the

---

† In the days of Confucius images were buried with the dead, and the "great master" predicted that eventually men would be sacrificed. His prophecy was verified, and men of ability became scarce. When Haji initiated a check on this terrible custom, great improvement took place. Native annotators on the classics note this,

common people, who often hang up pictures, locks of hair and other offerings as they would in the temples.

When a person is dying no prayers are said by him or his friends. But when the last breath of life has passed away, the body is moved with the head to the North and a white cloth is placed over the face. Word is then sent to the officers of the ward and the *Kannushi* of the *Miya* in the vicinity, occasionally, if not too far, to the *Ubusuna* of the deceased. The *Kannushi* performs the ceremonies for the dead called *Shokonsai*. A desk is placed near the head of the corpse on which lights and offerings are placed, generally salt, water, rice, saké, cakes, fish, fruit, dried seaweed, vegetables &c. The *Reijie* is prepared, consisting of a mirror, on the back of which the name of the deceased is written, and placed in a small tub, which is again covered with white material, and is, for the space of forty-nine days, daily supplied with offerings, and prayers are daily repeated before it by the members of the family of the deceased. Not sooner than twenty-four hours after death, is the body placed, by the immediate relatives, in a long coffin in a reclining posture—unlike the Buddhists. The *Kan*—coffin, made of *hinoki* or *momi* usually—has placed inside it a cotton quilt and a pillow of tea-leaves or chaff, and the corpse is robed in a shroud of white material shaped like the ordinary dress. With the body is placed a garment suited to the season, a girdle, a suit of full-dress, a head-dress, an overdress of the ancient pattern called *Ho*. Metals must be excluded, and the coffin is covered and put into an outer case called *kaku* and placed on trestles. The funeral cortège varies with the rank and means of the family, and upon arrival at the cemetery the funeral service is performed. Over the grave a small mound is formed and a square post fixed in the centre, on the front of which is written the name and age, and on the sides the date of death, the place of birth and other particulars. The grave is fenced in with a paling of bamboo or wood, and at the gate is placed a small *Tori-i* of rough wood stripped of the bark, and plants of the *sakaki* are placed at each side of it, and inside, a cherry tree is planted on each side.

Besides the *Rejie*, after one hundred days have elapsed since the date of death, the wood-post is changed for a pillar of stone. On every anniversary of the death there is a *Matsuri* held in the house of the dead, and on that day a visit is paid to the grave. Every year, during the third month, a day is chosen on which a ceremony is performed in honour of the ancestors of the family, and prayers are offered up and petitions for prosperity during the year. Again in the autumn, during the ninth month, a thanksgiving is held and again the ancestral tombs are visited, both sexes joining in these rites.

A rough outline only has been given of these rites and observances. To enter into fuller detail would demand more space than can now be spared, as other subjects demanding notice await attention.

BUDDHISM.

The native accounts, ordinarily received as correct, relate that Buddhist doctrines together with the appertaining idols, descriptive books &c, were introduced from Hakusai (Corea) in the winter of the year A.D. 552, being the thirteenth year of the reign of Kin mei Tenno, thirtieth of his line since the reign of Jimmu. The idols, books &c were given by the Mikado to his chief Councillor of State, Soga Iname, who deposited them in a part of his palace thenceforth named Kogen Jie (the temple facing the plains). In the year 577 the sixth year of Bidatzu Tenno, the successor of Kin mei the paraphernalia of the religion were again brought to Japan and its doctrines found favour at Court. In the fourteenth year of this monarch's reign—A.D. 585, a terrible pestilence raged in the country and a Councillor of State, Moronobe Moriya, expressed to the monarch his apprehensions that the visitation was sent expressly by the gods to mark their anger that the old faith should have been set aside by or alloyed with the doctrines of a new creed. He was, however, unable to gain full credence, though successful in obtaining an order that the rites of the new religion should not be celebrated. The temples were accordingly burned and the idols cast into the rivers. Hori ye in Osaka is one of the places still pointed out where this was done; he was afterwards killed during some local disturbance while supporting law und order.* Mayado

---
* This seems to have formed a very good precedent for the persecution of Christians exactly ten centuries later.

Oojie, who was cotemporary with Moriya, was an active disseminator of the new creed and is highly venerated by all the various sects. His *okuri-na,* or subsequent name, by which he is at present designated is Sho-toku-tai-shi (exceedingly virtuous son). Idols representing him in his teens, or as at the period of his decease, seated and crowned may be met with in nearly all the Buddhist temples. He was not of the priesthood and is the only layman on record as having been apotheosised.

The origin and history of Buddhism was soon disseminated through the medium of the Chinese literature which the priests received. They, or their disciples, would appear to have been the first to make use of the Chinese characters, Chinese writing not having been generally known at the date of introduction of the new belief.

In A.D. 624 two priests named Kan-ro and Taku-sek- arrived in Japan from Hakusai. The former was elevated to the rank of *So-jo* (chief-priest) and the latter constituted *So-dzu* (vicar-general). These were the first members of the priesthood to whom a grade was assigned by the Court.

In A.D. 700 Do-sho, an *O-sho* (chief-priest of a temple), died and was cremated, and this was the first time that cremation was practised in Japan.*

In A.D. 889 Uda Tenno, the fifty-ninth of his dynasty became a Buddhist priest taking the name Kam-pei-ho-o so called from the name of the year, in which he took

---

* Eleven and-a half centuries elapsed before it was prohibited by the present *Shosei* officials as contrary to the principles of Shintoism.

his vows. During this period nothing was definitely settled as to the various sects, or with regard to their conflicting views as to rites and observances.

Simultaneously with the dissemination of the principles of the new faith the schisms, which invariably arise when success and freedom from persecution have dissolved the bonds which unite co-religionists in periods of oppression, began to show themselves. Do sho, whose decease in the year 700 A. D. at the temple of Ko-fuku-ji of Nanto (South capital) in Yamato no kuni, we have already noticed, was *Kai-san* (opener of the hill), founder of the above-named temple and of the old Buddhist sect named *Ho-so* (knowledge of a myriad subjects.) The tenets of this sect were divided under five headings: the names of things; the forms of things; discrimination; true intelligence; form of the soul. There are older sects, but this took precedence of the others. The San-ron shiu, or sect of three arguments, is the oldest of these. It was founded in A. D. 621 by Yeka who resided in Igami-dera in Kawachi. Its tenets are divided into the following: the medium arguments, the hundred arguments and the twelve gates. As a sect it has become extinct, absorbed by some of the more recent developments. It embraced principles enjoining complete indifference to mundane affairs—in fact thorough personal nullification—and ignoring all action by its disciples.

In A. D. 735 Gem-ba-so-jo founded the sect known as *Gu-sha* the tenets of which were taken from the prayer-books of that name. They are comprised in 30 volumes. The temples in which these tenets were first imparted were known as *To-dai-ji* in Yamato and *Mi-idera* in Oomi. The principles of the sect are divided under two headings viz: the control of the passions, as selfishness, covetousness, &c., and the governance of the thoughts. This sect, or such portion of its tenets as have not died out, has also been absorbed by some of the more recent.

In A.D. 749 Do sho and Do ji proceeded to China and on their return thence brought with them a work on Buddhism, styled *Jo-jitz-ron* (the true argument) in twenty-seven volumes, and upon these tenets the Jo-jitzu-shiu was founded. Its principles taught the utter absence of substantiality in all things. Life itself was but a prolonged dream, the objects about us mere delusive shadows or mirage, the product alone of the imagination. This sect is no longer represented by priests or temples, such of its dogmas as survived having been incorporated with the tenets of other Sects.

In the same year Kochi Dai-so-dzu of Todaiji, Yamato caused a small temple to be built, and instituted a new Sect, that of *Ke-gon shiu*, or Conspicuous. The book in which the special principles which guided this Sect were found, were compiled by Ten-shin-bo-satzu of India, one of the original disciples of Buddha. It taught that the soul resembled a fair page upon which the artist might trace a design, and that special care was needed to prevent the impression of evil designs, in order to which the thoughts should be continually directed towards Buddha.

This sect, also, is a thing of the past, while many of its tenets survive, amalgamated with those of existing sects.

In A.D. 754 Kan-chi-osho of Sho dai ji in Yamato

was possessed of three thousand *shari*—the small pearl-like substance that remained after cremation of the Buddhist saints,—also certain books named *Gen gi* (original signification) *Mongu*, (rare and excellent collection ;) *Shikan*, (perpetuation of that which is admirable). These he presented to Shomukotei the 45th Mikado who accepted them with pleasure, and, together with four hundred and thirty four of the chief officers of his Court, became a pupil of the priest. In close vicinity to the Imperial residence a temple was erected, Kai-dan-in, where the *go kai*, or five commandments were first promulgated. These five prohibitions, or commandments of Buddha, are against *setzush*ı (destruction of lfe) ; *chiuto* (dishonesty); *ja in* (adultery); *mogo* (untruth) ; *on jiu* (wine-drinking). To these are appended six radicals : *roku kon* (eyes, nose, ear, tongue, body, mind) ; *roku jin* (six unclean things (valueless as dirt) color, sound, smell, taste, touch); maxim : the former of these to be kept under control; and not to be led into error by the latter. This is the *Ritzu Shiu*. In Uyeno, Yedo, there is a temple known as Ritzu In still in existence.

In Toodo, Morokoshi (China) at Tendaisan, Chi-sha-daishi taught the tenets of the creed afterwards brought over to Japan and thence known as *Ten dai shiu*, the accurate Japanese name being *Hok-ke shiu*. In the year 788 Dengiodaishi caused a temple styled Yen-riaku-ji, from the name of the year, to be erected at Hiyosan, on the boundary of the provinces of Yamashiro and Oomi. Here he founded his sect, and taught the doctrine of *Chin sha*, of which the leading principle is, that the teacher must thoroughly estimate the character and ability of his pupil, and in accordance thereto so apportion his instruction, within the range of his comprehension, that the pupil may not be hurried beyond it. These are the Jesuits of Buddhism. At Uyeno, Tokio the temple of Kan ye ji was erected by the Tokugawa for this sect in the year 1624 and thither devotees proceed to prayer on the 3rd 18th and 30th day of each month. Their common prayers are *Asa-dai-moku-yu-nem-butzu* and the more frequently employed *Namu-amida-butzu*.

In the year 813 Kobodaishi, the compiler of the present Japanese syllabary *I, Ro, Ha,* founded a temple at *Kon-go-ho-ji* at Koyasan in the province of Kishiu, where he taught the tenets he had learned in his travels abroad. He was conversant with much of the Pali, Sanscrit and Chinese literature, especially in Buddhist classics.* He also founded the temple Tou ji at Kugo in Yamashiro. The sect is styled *Shin gon,* or true words. Its principles taught that the subtle points of an argument should be seized and elaborated. It points out three paths to *jobutzu* (perfect bliss) which means absorption into Buddha.

Ringu no jobutzu or retention of detailed ways, so as to become *hodoke,* loosed or free (from earthly ties). On all sides are the six associated things, earth, water, fire, wind, air and mind—*Dai nichi niyorai*—(the same as *Ten*

---

* The *Devanagari* alphabet of 47 characters bears a strong resemblance to the *Bon ji*—priests' letters— of the present, and it may be fairly inferred that the I, Ro, Ha was formed on this plan for convenience at a period when Chinese was little known in this country except by the priesthood. *A gongio* is the name of the book of prayers from which the characters are said to have been taken arbitrarily by him for the foundation of the Iroha.

sho-ko of the Shintôists) and the multitude are alike possessed of these six things, the proper control and use of which lead to perfection.

Gaku-tai jobutzu, or second road to bliss, is by the observation of and deduction from the buddings of Spring, the bloom of Summer, the fall of the leaf in Autumn, the withering of the verdure in Winter; when looking over the earth in contemplating its vastness, when on the water its roundness, and when examining three-cornered objects, fire. By meditation and solitude to become eventually equal to *Dai Nichi Niyorai* in Paradise.

Zentai-jobutzu, the true way. The head is compared to the high mountain on which the saints assemble and the body to the sea which encircles it. Within the mind are seated the thousand worlds; multitudes of *renge*, (lotus flowers,) should spring therefrom. The body is likened to a mountain guarded by an iron fence, the mind resembles the broad seas and rivers; the head is like Benten tai Shaku, the chief of the saints in Paradise; the eyes are like Yemma-ho-o, god of Hades; the body like Shodai ten nin and Ten yo ten do, good action, and a multitude of *yembudai* (evil thoughts and deeds). In the sixteen large countries, the five hundred smaller countries and the countless others as numerous as millet seed (grains of rice being thereby inferred), there exist gods great and small, and in all things exist the five elements, earth, water, fire, wind, water. The correct observance of these things leads to annihilation and bliss through absorption into Buddha.

In 1596 Chishaku In of Higashiyama in Yamashiro

became the place of resort of followers of a subject of this belief known as *Shin-gi,* or new faith, founded at that place by Gen-yu-sho-ken-so-jo. The prayers used are: a long one commencing *On-abo-kiya* also *Namu-dai-shi-hen-jo-kon-go* from *namu* to pray and the title of the founder, and *Namuamidabutzu,* I pray to Amida Buddha.

These foregoing eight sects are the most ancient forms of Buddhist worship in this country. Their priests were forbidden to eat other than vegetable food. *Saké* also was prohibited and celibacy enforced. There were many forms of prayer common to all these sects, and that in most frequent use, *Namuamidabutzu,* was used by the disciples of each and all. It is related that the priests used mushrooms in order to simulate as closely as possible the flavour of fish, and that they showed much culinary skill in preparing dishes resembling the prohibited articles of diet. Of these Sects *Tendai* and *Shingon* possess numerous temples and multitudes of followers; *San-ron* and *Ritz* exist only in name and have no temples, and the other four are extinct, certain only of their peculiar tenets still surviving among those admitted by sects now flourishing.

In A.D. 1202 the *Zen shiu* sect was founded by Ye Saï at Kennin ji Kioto. Its professors teach that perfect tranquillity both of body and mind is essential to salvation. It is also styled *Butzu-shin-shiu,* or sect whose mind assimilates with Buddha, from whom it claims to have received its articles of faith direct. These are divided into two classes. The Inner teachings have certain proverbial expressions of their principles such as: maxims of doctrine are without rule; gain that without rule, for its doctrine cannot stand. *Riyo-jiu-bo-satzu* is quoted for these and other similar expressions, such as that emotions that leave no impression upon the mind or that cause neither anger nor satisfaction are naught, as also such things as possess neither beginning nor end. The exterior teachings are in their minor details somewhat antagonistic to the foregoing. They are subdivided into *jisso*, true form, and *muso*, formless. These teachings are styled *Kiyoje-betz-den*.†

Hoben, or parables, are of three kinds, used by the priests as a means of convincing their disciples. *Rihi*, negation, is the leading principle. *Kikan*, the mind, is but a machine: an ox of clay swims on the ocean; a horse of stone mounts to the skies. *Kosho*, that which has neither head nor tail. There are prayers, known as *rinzai* or *saika* and *soutou* in numerous volumes. This sect existed at Oobaku in China, and seeds of the faith were in time borne to Japan.

In the year 1278 at Nanzenji in Kiyôto, Mukanzengi taught a new doctrine known as *Rinzai*.

In 1655 at Uji Mampukuji Oobaku Ingenzenji established another offshoot professing the pure Oobaku doctrine.

In 1233 also at Uji Horinji Dogenzenji founded the more ancient branch of the sect known as *Soutou*. The priests are restricted to vegetable diet and are not allowed the use

---

† It is impossible to convey to the mind of the European in these brief notes a clear conception of the abstract principles which are mixed up with play on words in the rendering of the Chinese character. An effort, however, has been made to point out the more salient distinctions between the sects.

of *saké*. Celibacy is imposed upon them. The prayers are known as *Komiyo-shin-gon* (the brilliant unreserved words of truth) commencing with the words *On-abo-kiya* and the more familiar *Namuamidabutzu*.

The Jau-do-Shiu (Heavenward bound Sect) was founded in A.D. 1211 by Ho-nen-sho-nin at Kioto in Chi-won-in.

The temple at Shiba, Tokio, Dzo jo ji, was founded by Sei-so-sho nin, also a priest of this sect, in 1605.

The priests of this sect are forbidden marriage and wine and all but vegetable articles of food. The name of the Sect is taken from its belief in prayers to Amida Butzu, which are efficacious to ensure the devotee being reborn into paradise. Honen taught that whether the priests and their followers were learned and devout or the contrary mattered little as regards the final result, and that all that was really necessary was the incessant repetition of the prayer to Amida Butzu *Namu Amida Butzu*, (Pray to Amida Butzu), and accompanying this by hammering on a bell called *Fusho*. The solution of abstract questions and doctrinal controversies are not needed to promote the work of salvation. On the anniversary of a death, a rosary of one hundred and eight large beads is laid on the mats and the priest sits in the circle thus formed, the friends of the deceased sitting outside facing the priest, and, as they pray, passing the beads from left to right. This ceremony, which is called *Hiakuman ben*, is exclusively practised by this sect.

Two priests of this denomination used to be seen and heard in the streets, handsomely dressed, striking a small gong tied to the front of their girdle, and singing, or rather intoning their prayers. Women were in the habit of making them presents, as handsome men with fine voices were invariably chosen, until jealousy placed a check to the custom.

Jau do shin shiu, (the new road to paradise) a branch of the foregoing sect, was founded by a pupil of Honin, called Shin-ran-sho-nin in 1262. He was twenty-first in descent from his ancestor Amatzu-ko-yane-no-mikoto, and great grandson of Tai-sho-kan-kama-tari Nai-dai-jin, and son of Kodai kogu taishin ari-nori.

In 1400, the two large temples *Nishi* (west) and *Higa, shi* (east) Hongwan ji were founded in Kioto. Besides these there are two large temples similarly named in each of the cities of Ôsaka, Yedo, Nagasaki and Niigata, built on the same model.

The name *Ekko* is derived from Ekko-sen-nen-mu-rin Jibutzu, the name of a book of prayers, the everlasting Hodoke, which enjoins that the mind is to be thoroughly absorbed in the *nenbutsu* or act of prayer. This designation, though not recognised by the sect itself, has been applied to it on account of the singleness of purpose exhibited by the worshippers at their devotions. The name *Monto* (lity. concentrated within the gates) would seem to be derived from the fact of the sect being so undivided. The priests are permitted to marry and their diet is not prescribed by rule. To the accusation of uncleanness with which they are charged by other sects, they reply that the bright rays of the sun shine on all things alike, and that as there can be no difference in the eyes of the gods, the maxims and narrow-minded doctrines, with the neglect of which they are reproached, can only have proceeded from the folly or vanity of man. In place of selecting sequestered spots in the hills as sites for their temples, they build them in the centres of population and endeavour, by all means within their power, to attract the people to them.

Kanzewon Kuanon, goddess of mercy, assumes thirty-three forms, under which she protects the human race and permits her priests to be as other men. Self-inflicted penalties, penance, fasting, pilgrimages, isolation from society, whether as hermits or in the cloister, are not imposed by the pure Buddhist doctrine. Devout prayer and a pure life are alone essential to salvation from punishment in a future state, and in order to secure a place with Buddh.* Unlike the other Sects the priesthood is in this hereditary, the care of each temple being transmitted from father to son. Should the priest have no male heir, his daughter's husband, should he have a daughter, succeeds him. The priests and their families are said to possess higher erudition than that of other sects, and in periods of domestic broils, or war with foreign powers, form (like the monks of Spain during the Peninsular War) a clerical militia available for defence. The *Ofumi*, or writings, are daily read. These were composed by the founder Shinranshonin, and are written in *hiragana* so as to be intelligible to all. The altar is named *Omamukisama*, and is invariably gor-

---

* The sect is without doubt the Protestantism of Buddhism in Japan, and from the high position of its founders and followers, has taken a prominent rank in the religions of the country. It is this sect that is now agitating for separation from the Dai Kio In, so as to be at perfect liberty, and free of Shintô influence.

geous both in temples and private houses, a circumstance which has given rise to the saying "As handsome as a *Monto* altar." In the morning the men while praying, wear a small silk overall, the women a narrow strip of white cloth or silk round the head. This is named *tsuno-kakushi*, or horn-hider, and is worn in order that should jealousy or evil be present in their minds—a not unlikely circumstance—they should not appear before the *Hodoke* as *Han-ya* or horned demons.

In the year 1222 A.D. at Tojo, county of Nagasa in the province of Awa, there was born on the second day of the second month (exactly 2174 years after the death and cremation of Shakka) one who subsequently became Nichiren sho nin, the most exalted Nichiren, who sixty years later succeeded in establishing a new sect at Hon koku ji, Kiôto. His name originated in the story that his mother during her pregnancy dreamed that she had swallowed the sun, *Nichi*. The original *ha* (sect) called *Ichi* (single-minded), afterwards the *Sho-retzu-ha* (superior doctrine), was formed and was instituted at Shorenji in Kiôto by Nichi zo sho nin. Its principles are contained in the Hokke kio,—the blossom of (Buddhist) doctrine— a work in eight volumes, and are the truest of all. They prescribe self-examination and reflection upon the blessings vouchsafed to them as a chosen sect. This denomination is fond of controversy, reviling other creeds with sectarian bitterness. One of their common sayings is worth giving: They who mumble prayers fall into *Gigoku* (Hades). The *Zen shiu* are furies, the *Shingon* unpatriotic, and the *Ritzu* thieves and malefactors;—all other sects but ours are without end or aim. Bigots offend continually by employing opprobrious language in their reflections upon other sects. They resort more than other sects to superstitions such as charms, spells and amulets. Their prayer-books are very numerous and the commonly heard *Na-mu-mio-ho-ren-ge-kio*, with its noisy accompaniment of drum-beating, is used by them exclusively. The priests should be strict vegetarians, abstainers from wine, and observers of a celibate life. A revival meeting of this sect is a scene of noise and indescribable confusion, and the state of excitement some work themselves into often ends seriously and sometimes fatally. They are great pilgrims. Hori no ouche is the chief meeting place in the vicinity of Yedo—on the 13th of the 9th month.

Of the preceding, Tendai, Sanron, Ritzu, Shingon, Zen, Jaudo, Ekko, and Nichiren are the eight existing sects. There are, however, other sects, which are not recognised, as being of minor importance.

In the year 1278 A. D. Ugio-ha-itzuhen-sho-nin founded the Jishiu, or time sect, at Fujisawa in Sagami near Yokohama, and a temple there is named after him. The priests connected with the temple may be numbered by scores. They wander throughout the empire. There are offshoots, small temples in other localities: that at Fujisawa, however, is the parent church. It is said that when a priest of this sect dies the *renge* or *hasu no han* ι (lotus flower) in the temple garden blossoms, and this indicates that a vacancy exists, which the novice next in turn is called upon to supply. These wandering priests give to those they meet on their journeyings, a piece of paper on which the words *Roku jiu man nin' ketzujo-o-jo* are written. Their founder, it is related, once made a pilgrimage to Gongen in Kumano in Kishiu and prayed for some favourable augury. His prayer was answered in a reply, which is condensed into the foregoing Chinese. These words are printed, or stamped at Fujisawa by a priest, who lies concealed beneath a musquito net, the labels being passed in to him beneath this cover, tied up in ten packets, each consisting of one hundred. It is currently believed that but one impression is needed to penetrate through the entire package of one thousand, while the outside wrapping-paper remains unsullied by the process. Women who are obviously with child receive two of these labels, and the perspicacity of the *Hokode* is such that it is said that females who are unsuspicious of the fact that they are *enceinte* first learn their condition from the unerring discrimination of the holy man's followers, who can recognize the *Tamashi* (spirit) of one of their sect, returned to earth. These travelling "colporteurs" of Japan are restricted in their diet to buckwheat flour, sweet-potato and a few other articles of food. Millet, rice, wheat, beans, sorghum, fish, &c., are prohibited to the chief priests, and strict celibacy is enjoined.

Hatchi tatake is the name of an offshoot from the Shingon Sect, established in the year 952 by Fudaraku san at Rokuharamitzuji in Kioto. Kuyashonin made a wooden effigy of himself at a branch temple named Gokuraku In and placed it here. There is a group of eight smaller temples within the boundaries of the *ji chiu*, or temple grounds. No other temples of this sect exist. The priests allow their hair to grow, and do not tie it up. They are permitted to marry and are unrestricted in respect to diet. They divide their time between prayer and the manufacture of the little *cha sen* (lity., tea-stirrer, better known to the thirsty foreigner as "swizzle-stick.") These, during the twelfth month, they dispose of in their wanderings throughout the country, their wares being stuck in a bundle of straw which is tied on a long bamboo and borne on the shoulder of one of the party, while the air resounds with the noise of a small gourd and the inevitable *namam-namam-da-butsu*. On festivals or at prayer meetings the *nembutsu* are invariably accompanied by dancing and capers.

The *Yamabushi* is a sect of wandering priests who, though not absolutely mendicant, do not decline payment for any services within the scope of their profession which they may be called upon to render. Many of them have their defined walks, and pay periodical visits to certain districts. They are most frequently called in to pray to Kojin—the god presiding over culinary affairs—monthly, and to offer up prayers for the sick, absent relatives and good fortune. They look upon Fudô as their patron and pray to him continually. They blow the *hora no kai*, a conch, before prayer. There are two classes, one originating in the *Tendai* sect who are under the protection of the *miya* Shogoin (a relative of the Mikado). Their head-quarters are at Hagurosan, Hosan and Miidera. The other is an offshoot of the Shingon, are under Samboin no miya and frequent Hagurosan. In spring and autumn they retire to the hills of

Oomine and Kadzuraki, and observing certain minute regulations as to costume, side arms, *tatchi*, &c., ascend the mountain. Sick men are left to perish on the way if unable to keep up with the procession.

The Gannin-boz (*v'de* article Beggars, Strollers &c.,) are said to be an offshoot from the Yamabushi.

There is a sect founded by Fukezenji, styled Kiomuso, whose tenets resemble those of the Zen shiu, which is remarkable only from their having until recently (when its use was prohibited) worn the *tengai*, a basket-shaped hat which conceals the features. Its members passed from door to door, playing a *Shak hatchi* and receiving a few cash as their guerdon, for which their fans are held out. They do not speak, but after playing a few notes pass on in silence to the next house. The chief temple of this sect is in Kiôto and is named *Mio an ji*, or temple of light and darkness. That in Yedo is known as *Ichi-getz-ji*, or one-moon temple.

The temples of the sect became sanctuaries to the *bushi* (*samurai*) who had committed crimes, or feared the resentment of an enemy. The unusual head covering which concealed their features and the priestly garb protected them from harm when they went abroad. About fifty years ago this costume became the vogue, and some of the daimios, gorgeously apparelled, did not disdain to appear publicly in the disguise. Money, if placed on the face of a mirror and handed to the Kiomuso, was not accepted, as this was held to indicate a desire on the part of the donor to discover his features by their reflection. The new *régime* has wisely discountenanced the wearing of the hats and has declined to recognise the sanctuary of the temples.

NUNNERIES AND CONVENTS.

The chief of these in Kioto is a temple named Hon Ko In; that of Aoyama, Yedo is styled Zen Ko Ji. There is also one at Kamakura, and numbers of them exist throughout these islands. The convents are not devoted to any particular sect, being common to all. Celibacy is enjoined. The *bikuni*, or nuns, are drawn from all classes of the people, though some of the nunneries admit the wealthy only. There are no "Sisters of Mercy" and the nuns who are permitted to wander beyond the boundaries of the convent are usually beggars. Those of the Zen shin sect used formerly to wander about the country in crowds, but this is now prohibited. It is not uncommon for women who desire to separate from their husbands, but who fail to obtain their concurrence *(ri yen)*, to retire to one of these *onna dera* (females' temples) and, after three or four years residence to return to the world absolved from their former ties, and ready, perhaps, to form a new alliance.

The objects of adoration of Buddhists are numerous, and we give a few of those most generally known. Certain sects devote themselves to some more than others, and even temples of the same sect have special favourite idols of their patron Buddhist divinity or saint. There are no mediators or intercessors, as in the Romish form of Christianity.

Taishak-ten-o (Heavenly Emperor), is prayed to for success and protection in this life only, the future not being within the province of this and the other *kami* of the Buddhist. The principal day of worship is that called Koshin, a moveable festival, chosen when the characters *Kanoye* and *Saru* come together in the cycle, both representing the principle of metals. There was formerly no idol of this *kami*, but it is now represented by a figure holding a *tama* (globe representing the soul) in the left hand. The Nichiren sect are the most numerous devotees of Tai Shak.

Mari-shi-ten is the great patron of all persons, young or old, learning writing, reading, dancing, singing, or a trade. The common form of this idol is a figure standing on the back of a galloping wild boar. It has six arms and three faces. The boar being the last of the twelve zodiacal signs and preceding the first sign *Ne* on repetitions, implies 'before the beginning'—the three faces, the eyes and countenance tend to all directions. The six hands denote dexterity at all work. The day of the Boar, *Inohi*, is the day observed in his honour. The Nichiren sect chiefly affect this deity.

Bishamon-ten, the Heavenly protector of priests. The *bushi* or cavaliers of all sects regard this deity as their special patron, and pray to him to make them dexterous swords men, good horsemen, learned scholars and so on. The idol is a standing figure holding up in the left hand a pagoda which contains the souls of the devout, and, in the right, a naked sword to protect those souls. The day of the Tiger *Tora no hi* is his periodical festival.

Kangi-ten, (Heavenly joy of joys) sometimes called ***Sho-den*** (wisdom). The original idol was two figures embracing, signifying Isanagi and Isanami of the Shintô, but it is now a single figure. All sects petition it alike for wordly success, and it is said that the righteous devotee receives benefit for seven generations to come. The figure if boiled in oil, is supposed to be specially pleased. According to the means of the petitioner the priest continues this while the devotee prays; if for 21 days at a cost of 35 *riyos*; if for 14 days, 25 *riyos*; and for only 7 days, 7½ *riyos*. Should the offerings placed on the altar be eaten by another, the good fortune of the eater deserts him and cleaves to the person who made the offering. The devotees of the divinity do not eat *daiko (ratanus sativus)* in any form. *Tora no hi* is the saint day.

Ben-zai-ten (Heavenly goddess of capacity and ability). All creeds, and especially women, pray to this goddess for ability, attractiveness and wealth ; men pray for wealth, and actors and others who make their living by amusing the public never fail to visit the temples of Bentensama, which are usually found near the water, often on artificial islands in lakes or shoal water. The day of the Snake *(Mi)* is the general occasion for visits to this shrine. *Tsuchi no to mi no hi* is the day on which these characters of the cycle come together; this occurs every sixty days, and is a day specially propitious for paying visits to Benten, the combination being lucky. (Vide *Jik kan* and *Jiu ni shi* in the calendar). From this the snake is associated with Benten as the fox is with Inari, and pictures of snakes are found in numbers at these shrines, worshippers and petitioners being careful not to kill these reptiles, fearing the wrath of Benten. The reptiles are invariably encouraged to frequent these shrines.

Dai koku ten. There are several forms of this deity. The literal translation of the characters is "Great black Heaven." The most commonly known form is called *Makara dai koku,* the meaning of which is 'immensity of earth.' The form of the idol, which is in every house, is a short stout figure, on rice bags, wearing a cap, with a large sack on the shoulders, the mouth tightly grasped with the left hand, while the right holds a mallet. The moral of this form is, that human nature being prone to an excess of ambition, therefore low stature and a humble attitude most befit it. The cap partly covers the eyes to prevent them looking too high, and to keep them bent on the realities of life. The bag represents wealth, like the wind, difficult to attain and requiring its outlet to be firmly controlled. The mallet is an emblem of labour, by which alone the fruits of the earth can be obtained, and the bags of rice on which the figure is mounted denote the wealth to be acquired by adopting these precepts which raise the lowly above the multitude. Traders of all sects incessantly try to propitiate Daikoku, and he has votaries among all classes. Farmers, and even young ladies address their petitions to him for full purses or the means of adornment. *Ki no ye ne no hi* day of the Rat, is the great day at these shrines.

Fudo-son—(Immoveable honored (one). Some sectarians confound *Sosa no* with this Buddhist god, others believe it to be a purely Indian Deity.* This idol is generally seated, and always surrounded with flames, holding a naked sword in the right hand, with which to punish the wicked and terrify humanity into obedience, in the left a coil of rope, to tie up the guilty.

All sects pay adoration to Fudo, but most especially the Shingon and the Yamabushi regard him as their patron. Pilgrimages to and offerings at his shrine are generally by the friends of sick people. Penances, such as making the pilgrimage without clothing, standing under a spout of cold water, or abstaining from favourite articles of food, and lengthened total fasts are commonly resorted to in order to propitiate this deity. Miracles are reported to be performed at these shrines, the blind to see, the lame to walk, the deaf to hear and the dumb to speak. The shrine at Narita Shimosa, and at Meguro in the suburbs of Yedo, are two of the principal in the north-east of Japan. Women rarely pray to this deity or visit his shrine, as he has the reputation of being very rough and violent tempered.

Ni-wo-son, (Two honoured kings) the guardians of the right and left. These are always placed under the gateway, as may be seen at Asakusa, and formerly Shiba. The most celebrated are at Shiba-yama-mura in Kadzusa. The idols are erect figures with flowing robes; that on the right, facing the temple, is red, has the mouth open,

---

* The propagators of Buddhism endeavoured to amalgamate the Shinto *Kami* with the Buddhist divinities, as, in this instance, where the Indian idol is confounded with the Japanese god. There are evidently some traces of the Zoroastrian (fireworship) belief of India in this idol Persons wishing to bewitch their enemies invariably appeal to Fudo. to vent his wrath upon such as they wish injury to.

and represents the *Yo* or male principle of Chinese philosophy. That on the left is green; the mouth is firmly closed, indicative of silence, the female *In* principle. Small prints of these, pasted on the beam over the entrance of houses, protect them from burglars and thieves. Travellers on foot present large straw sandals, and hang them at those places. They also burn *Sen ko* (incense) and pray for pedestrian strength to perform their journey.

Yeb.su, is the same as that mentioned as the aftername of Hiruko, the cripple son of Isanagi and Isanami, and therefore the brother of Ten-sho-ko. He is represented seated on a rock by the sea with a fishing-rod and a *tai* (serr. mer.) in his arms, on his head a *yeboshi*—a black cap worn by persons of rank. Seekers after wealth pray to him, and his idols are in every house on the *Kamidana* on *butzu-dana*. Between Osaka and Kobe the temple at Nishi no miya is the most celebrated of those dedicated to this god. The 20th of the 10th month is the great annual festival in his honour.

Funadama gu. (Ship-jewel-shrine) This is the protectress of voyagers, and to her sailors pray for fair wind, a safe passage, or for help in the hour of danger or storm. Each vessel has its altar where homage is paid to her. The idol stands on a rock with two attendants, surrounded by the waves.

Atago gongen:—So called from a district called Atago near Kioto, and *gongen*, temporarily visible, and is the name of the shrines in which are adored jointly Isanami, Homusubi and Nichira who was the teacher of Sho Tokutaishi, the founder of Buddhism in Japan. These shrines are visited by petitioners for good luck and for protection against fire. Atago yama at Yedo—the hundred steps—is an offshoot of the Kioto shrine.

Akiha gongen. At Akiha yama in Enshiu there is a temple called Hôraiji, founded by San shaku bo, who afterwards became incorporated with Tengu. There are numerous shrines throughout the country, which are constantly visited by petitioners for protection against fire.

Kompira (metallic (like) protector (of the) multitude.) Sosano, the unruly brother of Ten shoko, and, later, Shutoku in, the 75th Mikado have been included among these deities. The Buddhists join to these the worship of Gubera tai-sho a deity of a similar class. The representation of these, as Tengu, is a mask with an enormous nose, and the shrines are generally on the tops of mountains. The tenth day of each month is the usual *matsuri* or festival and petitioners for good fortune, &c, especially mechanics, are very numerous. *Iwashi* (sardines) and *sake* are abstained from by frequenters of Kompira shrines—a breach of these observances produces direful consequences. Sailors pray devoutly to Kompira for protection from the elements, and stories of ship-wrecked people having been saved by Kompira coming to the rescue are numerous. The Shintô name for Kompira is Kotohira. The principal shrine is that called Dzo-dzu-san in Sanuki, to which numerous pilgrims resort throughout the year, especially in the spring.

Yuya-gongen is another branch of the Tengu family.

Shichimen (Seven-headed serpent) at Minobusan in Koshiu. Nichiren-sho-nin canonized this monster. Sick people or petitioners for good fortune visit the numerous shrines that are erected throughout these islands on the model of the above.

Water and earth from the small artificial lakes always to be seen in the temple grounds are considered certain cures for all ills, the water as internal and the earth as external medicines. Only the Nichiren followers believe in the efficacy of these things.

Kishi mojin. (The mother of child demons) steals young children and devours them. She had a thousand children of her own, one of which Amida Niorai took and hid it from her as a punishment for stealing and devouring other people's children, careful and fond as she was of her own offspring. Upon condition of giving up these cannibal propensities the child was restored and she was told to eat the fruit of the pomegranate whenever she longed for little children to satisfy her depraved appetite. Now small children are taught to pray to her for protection. The 28th day of each month is her periodical festival.

These are the principal *kami* of the Buddhists.

The following are *Hotoke*, or divinities in human form, mostly canonized apostles and disciples.

Amida Niorai, the divinity so well known to us as the Dai Butzu of Kioto and Kamakura, is the premier divinity of the Buddhist faith. Sometimes these idols may be seen standing, but generally they are seated on the lotus-flower. This god is considered to be so far above the common deities that it is of little use for common mortals to attempt to attract attention, or to intrude on the sublime and total unconsciousness to all mundane affairs in which Amida is enveloped. The 15th of each month is the appointed day for visiting this deity's shrine.

There are six places in Yedo and its suburbs where there are idols of Amida which are visited in spring and autumn when the days and nights are of equal length.

Yakshi Niorai, (Divinity of medicinal herbs.) Sick people petition this deity for restoration to health. Diseases of the eye are specially under the care of Yakshi. There are six other similar divinities of lesser importance.

Kan-ze-onbo-satz is one of twenty-five divinities who are supposed to be cognisant of all matters, and able to help petitioners in any manner expressed in their prayers.

Dai-nichi Niorai is the same to the Buddhists as Tenshoko to the Shintoists, and they are amalgamated under this title (Great Sun divinity.)

Ji zo bosatzu (Divinity of the ground.) Childless parents petition Jizo for assistance to bear offspring. Jizo idols are generally figures of stone standing. Some sitting on a lotus leaf, holding a long rod in the right hand, and globe representing the soul in the left. Salt is the most usual offering and *senko* are burned. Seki no Jizo in Isé is the principal shrine.

Seishi-bosatz. As the name implies, is a divinity of great power and authority.

Monjiu-bosatz. This name implies extraordinary ability in teaching.

Fugen-bosatz. The divinity of those who wish to excel.

Kokuzo-bosatz is credited with the ability to assist all devout people in succeeding in their walk in life.

There are twenty-five *bosatzu* in all, the foregoing seven as well as the *Kanzeon* are included.

Mioken-bosatz, or *Hokushin-mioken*, is the north star and is prayed to for good luck.

Aizen mio-o, or *Ni jiu san ya* (The Moon and a star.) The Chinese character have a meaning that allude to dyeing and dyers. The ceremonies take place on the 23rd of the month at night, and the priests of any sect may officiate. Aizen at Itabashi, north of Yedo, is the principal temple in this part of Japan.

Yemma dai-O (The King of Hades.) There are ten of these, all represented taking notes of the good and evil deeds of mankind. In the common pictures a large mirror is represented in which men's thoughts and actions are reflected.

On the 16th day of the first and seventh months, great numbers visit temples containing idols of Yemma—friends of the departed, anxious to relieve the souls in limbo, have prayers said by the priests, and Yemma is expected to "write off" misdeeds from his ledgers in proportion to the amount of prayers paid for—so say the bonzes.*

Shaka niorai; the founder of Buddhism who died 457 B. C. The day of his birth according to the Japanese calendar is the 4th day of the 4th month. An idol of the infant Shaka is placed in a small shrine decorated

---

* There is a common saying, *Jigoku no sata kane shi dai*: Judgments of Hades depend on money—alluding to the purchase of the services of the bonzes.

with flowers, and an infusion called *Ama-cha* is poured over the figure, a small bamboo tube being filled with it and carried home.

On the 15th of the second month, the anniversary of Shaka's death, pictures of the reclining figure of the Buddh are hung up, and on these pictures, all the saints and animals birds and insects are portrayed as in deep grief—the cat only is omitted.† There is a story told of the priest of temple of Nan-senji in Kioto, called Cho-den-su, whose cat asked him why his race was excluded and begged that the priest would put a cat into the picture, which the priest did, his pussy being a pet and very devout. This is the only picture of the sleeping Shaka with a cat among the mourners.

The founders of the various sects are represented by idols, and are principally adored by the followers of the respective sects they founded.

Hotei is the name of a celebrated Chinese priest, who was kind to children. He is the Japanese Santa Claus, and is represented with a capacious sack gathering good things for his little friends. He is said to have eyes in the back of his head and can see round corners whether little boys and girls are good or naughty.

Jiuro jin is a little man with a tall head, also known as *Fukuroku jiu*. This is intended to mean the South Star, or *Nan kioku*.

---

† A common child's tale as to the reason of the cat being excluded from the animals that surrounded the death-bed of Shaka is this. A rat being sent for medicine for Shaka, a cat sprang out and killed the rat; consequently, before the physic could again be sent for Shaka had died, and the death is attributed to the cat's killing the rat and delaying the medicine.

Of the foregoing, the following seven, Bishamon, Benten, Yebisu, Daikoku, Hotei, Jiuro, Fukuroku Jiu, are the seven gods of prosperity that sail in the Takara bune, or ship of fortune, coming into port on new year's eve.

Shotokutaishi, the first son of Yome tenwo. Nichira who came from Haku-sai, became his teacher, and he became a learned Buddhist scholar while yet a child. He was the founder of the religion in Japan and died at the age of 49. He has six names significative of his acquirements and ability.

Idols may be seen, well worn by devotees rubbing the figure and then the corresponding portions of their own bodies—this is called *Binzuru Sonja*, and represents this servant of the disciples of Shaka, noted for his energy and untiring perseverance in attending to his duties. (This "transfer by friction" is an ancient idea which our professors of animal magnetism might study with profit.) ‡

In all the figures the posture has a certain signification, and the idols are numerous, the same deity being represented in several attitudes and of various ages. The principal names have been noted, the others are divided into some scores of classes, each class containing groups of from five to forty individual idols. For instance, 7 *Kan won*, 6 *Jizo*, 33 *Dai kan won* and so on—not to mention the 500 *Rakkan* and other groups of disciples, *Bosatz*, *Shonin*, &c.

Chiu-jo-hime was the first Japanese nun, and the only

---

‡ Jizo, being scrubbed with straw and plentifully bespattered with water is frequently seen. It is considered a remedy for pains in the loins and extremities.

woman who is commemorated by an idol. She extracted the fibres from the lotus root, and wove them with silk, to make tapestry for altars.

There are twelve idols that nearly resemble our twelve signs of the zodiac—they are of Indian origin.

There are Buddhist gods, *Bosatz*, one for each of the thirty days in a month, and corresponding Shintô *kami* Daimio jin ‖ have been incorporated with them.

1st	Giogi bosatz ...	...Atsuta Daimio jin.
2nd	Tomio bosatz...	...Suwa Daimio jin
3rd	Toho bosatz ...	...Hiroba Daimio jin.
4th	Ashiuku bosatz	...Kehi Daimio jin.
5th	Miroku bosatz	...Keta Daimio jin.
6th	Namauto bosatz	...Kashima Daimio jin.
7th	Samauto bosatz	...Kitanotenjin.
8th	Yakshi bosatz	...Yebumi Daimio jin.
9th	Datsasho bosatz	...Kibune Daimio jin.
10th	Nichigetz bosatz	...Ten shoko Dai jin.
11th	Kangi bosatz...	...Hachimangu.
12th	Nausho bosatz	...Kamo Daimio jin.
13th	Kokuzo bosatz	...Matzno o Daimio jin.
14th	Fugen bosatz	...Ohara Daimio jin.
15th	Amida bosatz	...Kasuga Daimio jin.
16th	Dara ni bosatz	...Hirano Daimio jin.
17th	Jijin bosatz ...	...Obiye gongen.
18th	Kanzeon bosatz	...Kobiye gongen.
19th	Nikko bosatz	...Shoshin gongen.
20th	Gakko bosatz	...Kiakujin gongen.

‖ Late reforms have abolished the term *Dai miojin*, or great enlightened spirits, as applied to the Japanese or Sinto Kami.

21st   Mu jin i bosatz   ..Hachi O Ji gongen.
22nd   Semmui bosatz   ...Inari Daimio jin.
23rd   Daiseshi bosatz   ...Sumi yoshi Daimio jin.
24th   Jizo bosatz ...   ...Giwon Daimio jin.
25th   Monji bosatz   ...Seki san Daimio jin.
26th   Yakushi bosatz   ...Takebe Daimio jin.
27th   Roshana bosatz   ...Mikami Daimio jin.
28th   Birushana bosatz ...Hiosu Daimio jin.
29th   Dai nichi bosatz ...Mioga Daimio jin.
30th   Shaka Niorai   ... Kibi Daimio jin.

Sen nin, Spirits that haunted the mountains.

Onie, Demons.—These evil spirits are typical of bad actions.

Ten nin, Beautiful creatures from paradise,—really good actions.

Kariyobinga, Birds of sweet song in paradise making sweet music for the saints.

Temples were by custom the resting places of travellers, especially priests, and guests were entertained without reference to religious sect or creed.

Intermarriage and adoption frequently bring several sects into families, but this is tolerated; the temple in charge of the family grave only must not be changed, and in all grave yards are numerous tombs of people who have been born into families of different sects from that into which they were married or adopted and died in. Or the persons may of their own free will change their *Tera* to another sect and arrange to be buried in the grave-yard of the temple of the sect adopted. (This shows that there is much toleration and not a little laxity, although some sects quarrel freely.)

Hotoke is the generic term for the spirits of the departed that have become absorbed into the Nirvana which is the highest aim of the Buddhist. The divinities and household altars are usually known by this general term.

Niorai are the divinities who watch over humanity and to whom petitions must be addressed. Shaka is properly the only being that has existed on earth entitled to be called Niorai.

Bosatzu are the apostles of Shaka, and a few eminent priests of olden time, and are the chief patron saints of the various trades, virtues, views and wants of humanity.

Rakkan are the disciples of the Buddhist creed of the days of Shakka. There are the 16, the 500, and other numerous groups, all of India. They are not objects of worship, but only considered as holy men and patterns for priests especially.

The following are the purely Japanese grades of priesthood.

Ho-o is the name by which the Mikado is known if he enters the priesthood, as Uda Ten-O did, and the male children of a Mikado, who, with the exception of the heir apparent, frequently are obliged to take holy orders to prevent family feuds, were named Niudo Shin-O, or Ho Shin-O. The female children Niudo-Nio-O. Those Niudo who represented the Mikado were called Mia; for instance, there was formerly always one residing at Ouyeno in Yedo, the others were always in Kioto.

Monseki are the chief priests of the sects, and are appointed by the Mikado. As the Monto priests marry, the position remains in the family; if no children are born to them, adoption is resorted to. In the other sects marriage being forbidden, the place is filled by adoption. The Nichiren sect have no *monseki*. Common priests cannot attain this rank, members of the royal family being always appointed. The son or adopted successor is called *Shin Monseki*, (*shin* new; *mon*, gate; *seki*, mark), the successor to the royal patent as chief priest. If the *monseki* retires in favour of his successor, he is called *monshiu*, or *inkio* (recluse).

The teachers of the Emperor, if he enters the priesthood, are entitled to call themselves *Dai shi, Kokushi* or *Kai-shi* (the great kingdom, or the commandments-instructors.) The founders of *Shiu* or sects, are called *Kai-san* (expounder) and also *So shi* (first teacher).

Sonja (reverend persons) is frequently used in speaking of learned and holy men past and present.

Dai-sojo is the highest title of rank held by the priesthood and is equal to the temporal rank *Chiu-na-gon*. The next three grades in a descending order are *Gon-dai-so-ji, Dai-so-dzu* and *Gon-dai-sodzu*.

Shonin, or *hijiri-bito*, (a sage, a learned theologian) to whom the followers of his sect are indebted for much knowledge and extension of their creed.

Sho-nin, or most exalted; generally used when speaking of the founder or leader of a sect, especially when speaking of the *Son* or idol.

O-sho: the general term for superior priests.

Inge is the local chief of a temple (*Tera* or *In*) this

grade permits of a special dress being worn. Priests in charge of a temples of inferior grades are called *hojo, jiu-ii, in-jiu, anshiu* &c. according to circumstances. The inferior grades will be noticed hereafter.

Temples are generally built with money collected by the priest who afterwards takes possession of it. Some such as *Sen-yu-ji* have been built at the Mikado's expense; by the Tokugawa Shoguns at Nikko, the burial place of the first of the line, Iyeyasu or Gougen; at Kan ye'jie of Ouyeno, both held by priests of the Tendai shiu; also Dzo-jo-ji of Shiba, the priests of the Jiu-do-shiu. Daimios erected numerous temples at these three places. Temples attached to grave-yards are supported by the families who have relatives or friends buried there, from the prince to the peasant.

Until the last few years the priests drew large revenues from the Government and from high officials;—latterly they have been thrown on their own resources and become beggars literally.

The "monuments" of our country are here represented by little tablets on shelves in the temple building, before which offerings of food are made yearly, monthly or daily, in a style according to the donations to the priests for this purpose.

The idols on the altar depend upon the sect and fancy of the chief priest, and large temples are frequently surrounded with a cluster of smaller buildings containing special divinities erected by the devout as offsprings, when petitioning special favours in performance of some vow or as thanksgivings.

There are temples to which grave-yards are not attached. Such as for instance *Daishi* at Kawasaki; *Fudo* at Meguro; *Arai no yaku-shi, Awashima,* and Asakusa *Kanwon.*

The first visit to a temple is made sometime after the O-miya Mairi, and before the infants are taken to friends' houses, and on every new year of childhood, and on the anniversary of the death of near relatives. Temples are visited, in the grave-yard of which relatives have been buried,—if adopted or married into another family the temples and graves of the new relations must be visited as well. A newly married couple go to the husband's temple and graves together, and if the wife's family contains no males able to attend to her family tombs, the husband attends to them as well as to those of his own family. Nobles and high officials did not perform these rites at the same time as their wives.

Setzupo, the sermons of the Nichiren; *Hodan,* those of the Ekoshiu; *Dangi* those of Shingon and the others, are attended by both sexes of all ages and classes, except the aristocracy. Revivals, or *Kai-cho,* are common. They resemble the "*pattern fairs*" of Ireland, where the "patron saint" day gave excuse for a merry time.

Certain celebrated idols are frequently carried from place to place, and the temple chosen as the temporary abode becomes a centre of attraction. Some temples only display their treasures periodically, their *rei-ho,* relics such as *shaeri,* &c. or idols that work miracles. Occasional visitors can see these by money offerings to the priests. Temples and the grounds surrounding them are usually the playgrounds of the children of the neighbourhood, who do not seem to show much reverence to the holy places, nor to be much awed by the grim idols; nor are they troubled by the priests, unless some specially mischievous act is committed. Offerings of stone or metal lanterns, pictures, rice, *saké* and numerous other articles are brought to the temple by visitors and petitioners.

Kuji (nine figures). The charm used by many persons to protect themselves from harm. The fingers of the right hand are held in certain ways, and figures described in the air, then both hands joined, the fingers interlocked; after certain numerous set modes called *In wo musubu*, after which hot iron may be touched without injury, a naked sword edge may be stood upon, or robbers become rigid as if well bound with the thief-catchers' ropes. Small stones may be seen piled up in the lap of idols or on the top of *Tori-i* at Shintô shrines; this seems to be in allusion to children's departed spirits piling up stones in the other world.

Buddhist Obsequies.

Old people of either sex prepare for the approach of death by making frequent visits to the shrines of Hodoke and Amida Niurai, especially the latter. They also receive frequent visits from priests who preach and engage in prayer, thus "making their peace" and paving their road to paradise. Suicides prepare for death by appeasing the deities' just wrath at taking life, although their own. If people of means, the priests are introduced, and after the official inquest

has taken place all is made pleasant for the soul of the deceased, and the peace of mind of the survivors *(see Article "Suicide" et seq.)* When an accidental injury, or illness occurs the priest is sent for and the sick man's friends make pilgrimages to pray for his restoration. When this is despaired of, the invalid is again visited by the priest, who after his decease selects the *Kai-mio*, or posthumous name, and writes it upon a slip of white paper, pasted on a small tablet of unstained wood. In the meantime the deceased has been moved so that his head is turned to the north, and a folding screen, turned upside down, is placed there. A new desk about a foot in height occupies the space between the head of the corpse and the screen, on which cakes of raw rice-flour, called *makura-dango* (pillow-dumplings), are laid out as also a single rush wick, lighted, in a saucer of oil, with a saucer of unglazed ware in which *senko* (joss-sticks) are placed singly. The eating-tray, cups, saucers and chop-sticks used by the deceased are filled with vegetable food and placed at the side of the corpse, the latter on the left, or wrong side of the tray. Forty-eight hours after death the corpse is arranged for the *kan* (coffin) by ablution with warm water, the cold water being first placed in a tub and boiling water added.*
Unless the deceased has otherwise directed, the head is shaved, the priest while he is reciting certain customary prayers making the first three movements of the razor which he afterwards relinquishes to a servant. The corpse

---

* In consequence of this custom with regard to the dead warm water is always poured into a vessel first, the cold being afterwards added. The Japanese dislike to pour hot water into cold.

is then dressed for interment, the shaven being clothed as priests, the unshaven in ordinary dress. In all cases the shroud is white, of silk, linen or cotton and of the same make as the common outdoor dress of the deceased, the wealthy being attired in the same number and pattern of dresses as they wear in that season on gala or official occasions—a full dress, in fact, but entirely white. The hair of the females, when not shaven, is tied behind and falls down loose (as in the pictures of the ladies of the Court), and stockings are either put on their feet or placed in the coffin. Clogs or sandals, however, are discarded as they are not worn in paradise. The body is then placed in the coffin in the usual sitting posture, the hands of the shaven being joined as in the act of prayer. The *kan* (or coffin) are of various kinds, the commonest being the *haya-oké* (quick tub)—next in order comes the square box or an inner and an outer box of unstained wood, pine or *shinoki*, *(retinospora obtusa)*, the latter wood, considered the most suitable for sacred purposes, being commonly used by such as can afford it.

Earthenware jars are also used by the nobility and the wealthy. The better classes fill in the vacant space of the coffin with chaff, tea-leaves or the more costly *makó* incense, the highest ranks using vermilion. Those who are shaven have a cap placed upon the head. The bier is then laid upon trestles, the face of the corpse being turned towards the north, and a temporary altar is raised upon which offerings are placed as before.

The people of the house of mourning do not retire to

rest the night before the funeral, which is occupied by the priests of the family temple in reciting prayers. Until within the past few years the funerals of the well-born usually moved from their houses in the following order: Priests in a *norimon*; two white lanterns; trunks *(hasami bako)*; lance-bearers; retainers; halbert-bearer; incense-bearer; tablet (*ihai*) with *kai mio;* the coffin on a stand supported on two parallel poles, at the right the long sword of the deceased, at the left the short, both tied up in covers and borne by his highest retainers; the *dzori-mochi* (sandal-bearer); more *hasami bako;* a led horse, usually his favourite, the tail being cut short as a sign of mourning.† To these follow men bearing baskets of rain-coats and more retainers on horse-back or *norimon* or on foot. Then follows the heir on horse-back or in a *norimon* followed by the family and friends who have previously been invited, the *samurai* being dressed in *kamishimo* or full dress, and bareheaded and the bearers clad in white. Among the train are numerous bearers of lanterns, all of these being of white paper. Where possible every article is white or is covered with white paper, cotton or silk.

Upon arrival at the temple, where preparations to receive the *kan* have already been made, prayers are recited. The ceremony varies for each sect and is, besides, regulated by the wishes of the survivors, and their expenditure of money on display. The *indô-michi-hiku*, or guide to the road, is the chief portion of the ceremony. The prayers being ended the body is carried to the grave, accompanied

---

† Horses' tails are never docked under other circumstances.

by the priest who recites prayers until the interment is completed. In cases of cremation the body was formerly removed to the cremation-ground without further ceremony.

The funerals of towns-people, which are all on foot, are conducted with less pomp. First comes the priest followed by the coffin borne either in a *norimono*, styled a *nai só*, or private funeral, or on a platform with two poles by which it is carried on the shoulders of four or more bearers, the coffin being covered with a *tengai*, or small temple-like frame. Clothing of a white material is also placed upon the coffin. Singularly-shaped hats, made of rush, and woven in an open-work pattern are worn by the followers, who are dressed in *kamishimo* with short swords in their girdles.

The poorer class often bury their dead by torchlight to avoid the exposure of their poverty.

To return to cremation. The grave-yards are the same, but the tombs are made only to contain small jars in which the ashes of the dead are placed and labelled. There were various modes of cremation in use. First the coffin with its contents might be burned; this, however, was expensive. In the next the body only was placed in a separate compartment. And the cheapest and most common mode in use was to form a long pile of wood on which the bodies were placed in a row, with tickets to indicate the spot at which the ashes might be collected. The employés of the cremation-ground performed the necessary functions, a few only of the nearest relations attending to witness the preparations. On the lighting of the funeral pyre they took their leave, returning the following day to collect the ashes which they gathered with a wooden and a bamboo stick serving as tongs.‡ The small jars are of unglazed red ware, varying in size from 6 to 12 inches square. Sometimes the ashes were divided into parcels, a portion being sent to the various temples of the family, as by intermarriage its members would have relatives buried at several. Many who could afford the expense sent the jar with its contents to the Kobodaishi Temple at Koyasan in Kishiu, where an immense collection from all parts of the Empire may be found.

The periods of mourning, or *Kibuku*, are

For parents 50 days of *ki*, or deep mourning, during which business must be foregone and the use of the razor, *saké* and other than vegetable diet abstained from, and the temple and grave of the deceased visited daily. Other *tera* or *miya* must not be visited, the mourner being unclean. *Buku* are twelve months of mourning and uncleanness which follow death, during which the *Kami* may not be visited.

Brothers, sisters, husbands or wives, uncles, aunts, and all first-born children are *ki* during 20 and *buku* during 90 days; other children are *ki* for 10 days and *buku* for 45; cousins *ki* for 3 and *buku* for 7 days. But for the children of the mourner and cousins under seven years of age the prescribed term for *ki* is one day only.

---

‡ Hence the use of chopsticks, one being of bamboo and one of wood, is objected to as "uncanny."

Future State of the Buddhist.

There are ten *kai,* or states of existence, named by the priests of the various sects, viz : *Hotoke* the highest state of bliss or absolute nihilification.

Bosatsu, disciples of Buddh who exist in *Shim'sen* where they await absorption into *Hotoke.*

Yengaku, probationary to admission among the *Bosatzu,* and *Shómon* on the road to paradise.

Tenjio, the normal state of ordinary sinning humanity not actually guilty of any great sin.

These are the five states of the good.

Ningen or state of existence upon earth.

If a good and devout liver the soul goes to Tenjio and successively works up to the highest state or *Hotoke,* but if a person of indifferent life, a scoffer at religion or a brawler and blood-thirsty man, his soul flies to *Shiura* the place of perpetual quarrels and slaughter, the purgatory of the Buddhist.

If guilty of uncleanness or inhuman conduct such as Adultery, Rape, Incest or eating forbiden food, the soul after death is punished by the great judge Yemma by transformation into a beast and condemned to live on earth. This is the state of *Chikusho,* or transmigration of the soul into inferior animals, birds, reptiles, &c. *Gaki* is the punishment of perpetual hunger and starvation, and *Jigoku* (abode of beasts), pandemonium.

There are eight modes of torture. In *Tokatsu* the wicked are alternately beaten to death and resuscitated. In *Bakujo* the wicked are dragged limb from limb, chopped to pieces, pounded in a large mortar, sawn or planed into various shapes, as if by carpenters or mason's tools, the eyes are gouged, and the tongue or nails plucked out. In *Shingo* the crowd of the wicked are beaten about like potatoes in a tub. Then we have *kiokan* weeping; *dai kiokan*, great lamentation ; *shonetzu* and *dai shonetzu*, burning and roasting ; hills covered with large needles over which the wicked are driven ; lakes of fire and blood and brandings with red-hot iron and tearing the flesh with red-hot pincers. Also *muken*, or being thrown into the bottomless pit of perdition.

The chief of Hades, Yemma, has four executioners who carry into effect his sentences of punishment, *Semeru Onie*, Torturing demons ; *Dze sho me po*, executioner and torturer of the living, who is red ; *Sho gio mu jo*, green and *Sho metz metz i*, black, both torturers. *Ja ku metz i raku*, slaughterer, flesh-coloured. § The friends of the departed who are not aware of the sentence of Yemma must draw their own conclusions as to the destiny of his soul and therefore pay the Bonzes ‖ to pray for it. This is independent of the periodical visits of the mourners. The doctrine of the transmigration of souls leads all devout Buddhists to treat inferior animals humanely. Were it not for this it is certain that they would receive little consideration.

If the *hoji*, or prayers for the soul of the departed, be continued they will eventually succeed in bettering the

---

§ Those who stint the measure of food are condemned to perpetual hunger.

‖ Boz, or as pronounced by us bonze, or bonsan is derived from *Bo*, a temple and *dzu* master.

condition of the sufferer in purgatory, but this much depends upon the piety of the living. The stories founded upon transmigration are very numerous, and the charms, prayers and stratagems resorted to by the living to release the souls of their relatives, or by the spirits to stimulate the flagging efforts of those on earth are exceedingly interesting.

Gohu-raku, perfect felicity. These are as before named the five states from existence on earth to *Hotoke.* In the abode of the blest are ever-flowering, beautiful trees, fruits, song-birds, music, a delicious climate, and all that men call joy and ease upon earth. Those whose spirits are on the road to paradise do not need their friends' prayers, rather do their friends pray to them.

Childrens' spirits remain in *Sai no kawara,* the pebble plain (from *kawara,* the dry, gravelly bed of a river, of which there are many in Japan of great width). Here the little people employ themselves in making piles of stones which a mischievous demon ever and anon comes round to destroy. Those who succeed in raising a large pile attract the notice of *Jizo-sama* who causes their spirits to enter an unborn child and thus gives them another chance of living to puberty and by their own exertions securing happiness in a future state.

The unmarried of either sex, should they escape perdition, can only look forward to joining the children, as by the neglect of their duties to humanity they lose all claim to a home in paradise.

The soul must pass over the *Sandzu no Kawa* (the river of the three paths, the Japanese Styx) whence stretch out before it the three paths to Paradise, Humanity and Perdition. On the further side of the river an old hag *Shozuka no obasan* examines the passengers, points out the road they should follow, examines their garments— sometimes washing them as in the case of women who die in childbed¶—and when she sends them to Pandemonium unceremoniously strips them. The souls rescued by purchased prayers from Hades must enter the body of new-born infants and live again on earth, thus obtaining one more chance of becoming *Hotoke*.

The friends of the deceased must visit the temple and the grave on the seventh day after death and every seventh day seven times uninterruptedly. On the seventh day prayers are recited by the priests when the period of strict mourning is thus concluded. On this day the presents to mourners are reciprocated.

On the hundredth day the next ceremonial visit is paid to the temple before which the tombstone should be erected.

The next is the anniversary visit succeeded by the third, seventh, thirteenth, seventeenth (the Tendai sect observes also the twenty-seventh,) fiftieth, hundredth, and every fiftieth anniversary are all observed. *To* , or laths, with Sanscrit and Chinese characters are placed on the graves on the periodical visits of the visiting relatives,

Other details are now omitted which will find their

¶ Nagari Kanjo. *See* "Our Neighbourhood." Women who die in childbed are supposed to fall into *chi no ike* (lake of blood). When the out spread cloth breaks the bonds of purgatory are loosed.

place in our account of family and household matters. To conclude with a common proverb:

Gigoku no sata Kane Shidai. "The affairs of Hades depend upon money."

"HAKAMA AND KAMISHIMO."

On their arrival in Japan foreigners always noted the wide pantaloons, and associated them with the swords borne by the officials, deeming both of them badges of gentle condition, or of official rank.

There are at least eighteen different forms of this nether garment which should be noted *seriatim*. It is first worn by males in the fifth year, and there is quite a little family excitement on the occasion. This is usually the 15th day of the 11th month of the year in which the "young master" attains his fifth year, and is ceremoniously endued with these garments. The *ubusuna* (patron's shrine) is subsequently visited.

The *Kamishimo* (*kami*, upper; *shimo*, lower) which constitutes the old ceremonial costume of the middle classes and is the wing-like overall matching the *hakama*, is worn on this day by the boy and his friends, as on other special occasions. Tradesfolk and mechanics wear the *hakama* on special occasions only, such as marriages, funerals, new year's visits and the like, but do not wear the *kami shimo*. The respectable householders wear *hakama* on the occasion of visits of ceremony or official business, and the *kami shimo* or special occasions including anniversaries and visits to temples.

The general pattern of the *hakama* is a small striped design of sober colours, brown (*cha iro* or tea colour), greens, blue with a little red at times and generally some white, in a variety of styles. The material ranges from heavy and expensive silk *kohaku* or *sendai hira* down to *k kura*, cotton, and, of late, the cheaper foreign stuffs. *kohaku* is only used by the nobles of the higher class; *chabujima* and *sendai hira* by the aristocats; *tango jima, go sen hira, kawagoie hira* by the officiers, *kokura* by the *samurai*. the material differs little with the season, but the winter dress is lined for warmth; a thin material was sometimes used, but was not considered correct or officer-like.

Kami-shimo are usually made of *moro* (linen), sometimes of silk and linen, occasionally all silk well stiffened with starch. The stuff is generally light-blue or brown, dyed in a small pattern on a white ground, with the family crest on the back and shoulders, either that of the wearer or his feudal lord.

Sashi nuki is a *hakama* worn only by the courtiers; it is baggy at the lower extremities, generally purple or green with a large white pattern; the material is a thin satin with the pattern woven in the material.

Nobakama is similar in shape to the above, but is thus called when worn by the inferior officers of the court.

Okuchihakama is usually either white or red, worn by young nobles (*kugeshi* and *kazoku.*)

Kukurihakama is gathered in round the ancles and used or special occasions—generally under armour—by the nobles. The material and pattern vary according to fancy; the former is generally very expensive. *Naga-hakama* (long *hakama*) worn formerly by the *daimios* and *hatamotos* at the Shôgun's levees, on new year's day and other special ceremonials, marriages, funerals &c.

Tsugi-gamishimo is the ordinary *hakama* worn with a *kataginu* or overall of *ro* (silk gauze) of black or other colour, as a kind of undress costume for officers of all classes on duty, and is a grade more 'dressy' than the ordinary *haori* or overall jacket. This style was introduced about A. D. 1500 by Matznaga Danjô of Kioto, a retainer of the Ashikaga Shôgun, Yoshiteru. *Hira-baka-ma* is worn by all classes, and generally a *haori* with it. This is the most common form of the *hakama*; the colours are usually sober and the material inexpensive.

Ma nori bakama, as the name denotes is the riding dress, and therefore longer in the leg, and has stiffening in the seam which is called *semi* (locust) from its giving the garment a spread-out appearance like a locust's wings.

Matchi taka bakama is the same as the above without the *semi,* and is worn by gentlemen.

Fun gomi—a tight-fitting style mostly of expensive and gaudily coloured material, worn by officers at fires, by gentlemen travelling &c. sometimes with a velvet edging.

The *Yoshitsune bakama* is short, only reaching to the calf of the leg with a running string to draw it tight, worn by travellers and formerly under armour.

Soboso is like *fungomi,* but narrower in the lower part.

Hoso bakama is tighter fitting than the foregoing, and was worn by the soldiery before the introduction of foreign style. The *Tutchi tasuke* is like our knickerbocker and is worn with leggings (*kiyahan*) by the common people only.

Karusan is the *Tatchi tsuke* and *kiyahan* in one.

Hi bakama, scarlet *hakama* worn by the Empress, the concubines and ladies of the palace, the material varying with the rank, the colour the same for all. *Seigo*, a heavy material of raw silk worn by the Empress, is the finest. The others are of various qualities of silk. Latterly camlets and foreign goods have been used by the lower grades of palace female attendants.

Girls wear *hakama* occasionally, the hair being then dressed like a boy's, the sleeves of the dress being worn very long. Of late the pupils of girls' schools may often be seen weary *hakama*, over their ordinary robes.

Suicide.

Females who have resolved upon committing suicide commonly resort to a river, or not infrequently a well, and after deliberately filling the wide sleeves of their dresses with stones jump into the water. The most frequent motive for this act is the sense of their shame and the desire to conceal it; but it is caused not seldom by lovers' quarrels, by the dread of the loss of their personal charms through age or illness and, in the case of *geishas* and courtesans, often arises from the cruelty of their task masters.

Men who are heavily in debt, or crossed in the tender passion, are known to destroy themselves by drowning.

It is by no means unusual (and the native newspapers

chronicle such occurrences punctiliously), for a fond but disappointed pair of lovers to bind themselves together and thus to seek in their watery grave an union which had been refused to them in this life. This mode of death is styled *Shinjiu*.

Hanging is less resorted to by women as a mode of destruction—a singular parallel to the horror with which it is viewed by women in Europe. On the other hand it would appear to be frequently selected by men bent upon ending their lives. Trees are pointed out on which numbers have hung themselves, and it is related that they have the power of attracting their victims to them by some fatal power of fascination. A story is told of a vendor of lamp-oil who, on his rounds, passed beneath one of these vampire trees which stood on the site of the present Foreign College of Yedo at Kanda Bashi (then called Go-ji-in ga hara from the name of a temple that was once situated there) and felt an irresistible inclination to hang himself. A passer-by caused him desist, and he proceeded on his rounds. On his return, however, he was attracted to the same spot to find to his amazement, another man suspended from the tree and already dead. The frightened *abura-ya* hastily ran away, leaving his oil tubs at the fatal tree.

Some years ago at Kumagaye, about two days journey from Yedo, a guilty couple who could neither marry nor live together, resolved to end their lives by committing *Shinjiu* by hanging, and appointed a rendezvous at night for the purpose. On their meeting the man climbed a tree and throwing one end of his rope over a branch and the other round his throat, desired the woman to fasten herself to the loose end. The man then abandoned his hold upon the tree, and much to his surprise found himself upon the ground having, in his descent, hoisted his companion into the branches. Bethinking himself of the folly which could have prompted him to sorash an act, he unloosened the rope from his throat and turned homewards. Before he had proceeded far, however, he to his amazement met his sweet-heart, who showed equal surprise at meeting him, as she also had found suicide to be a mistake. They returned together to the tree, where they found a badger which had assumed the woman's form. Hanging is known as *kubi kukuri*. There are several *kubi kukuri* trees in Yedo.

Ji-gai. Men rarely cut their throats but women frequently resort to this mode of self-destruction, using for this purpose their razors or, if gentlewomen, their dirks, and there are stories of women who have slain themselves with hair-pins or *hibashi* tongs. About the year 1680 the fifth Shogun of the Tokugawa line, Tsunayoshi, paid a visit to Yanagisawa and fell in love with the *Okusama* (wife) of the latter. She was at the time enceinte, but her husband succeeded in persuading the Shogun that the child was his. As it proved to be a male a revenue of one million *koku* and the fortress of Kai were settled upon him. Ii Kamon, (ancestor of the Regent), conspired with the Midai sama of the Shogun to assassinate Tsunayoshi before he could place a false child in the exalted position intended: she cut the Shogun's throat while he slept and subsequently cut her own.

Innumerable instances of this mode of suicide are furnished by all ranks, jealousy being the most frequent motive. A gentleman sent his wife home to her family in disgrace. He was an old man, she a young and beautiful girl. Prior to her being coerced into marriage she had had a lover, who continued visit to her in the old man's absence. The latter however discovered their intimacy, slew the gay Lothario, and sent the guilty survivor to her parents' home. On her way home she succeeded in killing herself with the tongs of a brazier, which a servant managed to slip into her *Kago* unperceived, and when she bearers arrived at her home, their fair burthen was no more.

The notorious *hara kiri* is a common mode of suicide, differing from the official or judicial method. Here the man (for women never rip themselves open) holds the small knife in the left hand and cuts from right to left across the abdomen, beneath the navel, eight inches and continues the cut upwards three inches.

A skilful surgeon in Yedo succeeded in stitching together the abdomen of a *samurai* who had ripped himself up, but, during a thunder storm which occurred shortly afterwards, the stitches gave way and the patient died.

The writer remembers a young gentleman who being suspected by his uncle of a guilty intimacy with his young wife was peremptorily chassed. The young man proceeded to the house of the family physician, and while left alone for a few moments succeeded in ripping himself up. On overhearing the intelligence of his death his paramour killed herself by biting her tongue, a common mode of suicide with women.

The subject of suicide in this country might be enlarged upon to a greater extent than the proportions of these notes admit. We will, however, notice a few of the earlier and most celebrated cases.

In A.D. 313 the fourth and fifth sons of O-jin-Ten-O (afterwards known as Hachiman sama) had a dispute about the succession to the Throne, each declining the honour in favour of the other, and finally, after three years of debate, the fifth son, Waka irako no mikoto, committed suicide by cutting his throat to make way for his brother who became Nin toku Ten-O.

In A.D. 671 Otomono-Oji attempted to assassinate his nephew, Oieno Tenchi Ten-O,* and failing, hung himself.

In 1170 Yoritomo's uncle, Tametomo, was defeated at Idzu by the Heké, when he disembowelled himself, and then cut his own throat. This is one of the oldest cases of *seppuku* on record. Ten years later Yorimasa failed to depose Kiyomori, and committed suicide by *seppuku* at Bioto-In in Uji.

In 1289 Asaharu Tameyori rebelled, and, being defeated, was ordered to commit *seppuku* in the official palace (Shinden.) This is one of the oldest instance of judicial suicide, *i.e.* by order of the Government in expiation of crime.

In 1357 a priest named Yegen rebelled against the Ashikaga Shogun Takauji, and being unsuccessful, poisoned himself.

---

* The same Tenchi Ten-O, was the author of the first poem of the Century of Poets (see Mr. Dickins Japanese Odes and other Translations.)

There are but few instances on record in Japan of suicide by poison, although a Chinese custom, and likely to be adopted by scholars of the classics. The poisoning of enemies or opponents, however, was common.

In 1586 the lord of the provinces of Noto, Niwa Nagahidé, who was subject to spasmodic fits, killed himself by disembowelment, to free himself from the excruciating pains he suffered.

In 1591 Hidetsugu, having been accused of plotting the assassination of his uncle Hideyoshi (Taiko) who had adopted him as his son, escaped to Koyasan in Kishiu, and, failing to prove his innocence, chivalrously ripped himself open.

The judical *Seppuku*, by order of the Government, seems to have been a recent custom, indeed, does not seem to have obtained previous to the time of the Tokugawa dynasty of Shoguns. The most celebrated case is that of Asano Takumi no kami, as a punishment for drawing his sword in the palace, A.D. 1699, when, in a fit of anger and jealousy, he attacked and wounded Kira Ko'skenoske. †

Officers of the Government or of the Daimios were sometimes obliged to expiate the faults of their lords, and these occurrences form the foundation of innumerable tales of loyal and brave men of all times, past and present.

Women have rarely been known to hang themselves. A case of a female who died not long ago of self-inflicted *seppuku* was remarkable and unprecedented in native

† This forms the story of the forty-seven *rônins*, so well told by Mr. Mitford, and a translation of the piece as put on the stage appeared in the *Far East* 1873-4.

annals, and there are no cases known of persons being murdered by disembowelling.

When a man's honour has been wounded by persons physically superior or of higher position, the injured man not unfrequently first kills his family, wife and children even, and then commits *seppuku,* leaving behind him a written statement of his wrongs, which then become known to the authorities, and stringent means are resorted to in order that justice may be done to all parties.

Suicide by fire-arms is unusual. Fire-arms are not generally possessed by the Japanese and are never loaded but when out shooting, which is not a common pastime, even few of the high officials caring for it, as hunting is a means of livelihood and almost a hereditary trade. But latterly since foreign drill and arms were introduced, occasional cases have occurred of death self-inflicted with fire-arms, the muzzle of the weapon being placed against the breast, and not the head, as is more common with foreigners.

There are many legends of faithful followers being forced to commit *seppuku* by other disloyal retainers— the axiom 'dead men tell no tales' being well understood in Japan. Warriors beaten in the field often committed *seppuku* in preference to flight, and the wounded invariably themselves put an end to their misery, or got some friend to sever and carry off their heads.

Amongst the common people, poverty, discovered dishonesty or other disgrace often leads them to put an end to their lives by hanging or drowning; men principally by hanging themselves, women by drowning in a river or even a well. Lovers vow to die together either by drowning or by the man first killing the woman by cutting her throat, and then committing *seppuku*.

Men rarely cut their own throat, or poison themselves. Those who drown themselves are usually old men. Women of determined character, if they have no opportunity to drown themselves, cut their throat.‡

From time immemorial it has been, and still is, the invariable custom on the occasion of a wedding in the higher classes of society that the bride is provided with a lacquered box, about the size of a small lucifer box, in which are placed two dried beetles, of a golden colour, known as *Tama mushi* (jewel insect) which, if swallowed, are supposed to cause speedy death. This is in case something should happen to make her wish to put an end to her existence.

There are few cases, however, in which these means have been resorted to, and the real poisonous insect is, it may be credited, rarely placed in the box.

Although accidents by fumes of charcoal are common with foreigners in Japan, they are rarely heard of as occurring to natives, and suicide by asphyxiation with charcoal fumes is practically unknown to the compiler of these notes, notwithstanding much enquiry, and a personal experience of over a decade in Japan.

Biting the tongue is resorted to by women mostly, but men have been known to attempt it, for instance, when deprived of the use of their hands or instruments, as

---

‡ Women, married and single, always have razors in their toilet furniture, often in their pocket dressing-cases.

when in the hands of the police—with women, too, when tied up by villains in attempted outrages.

Setzupukku,* pronounced *seppuku*, also means *hara kiri* or abdomen-cutting. When ordered by the Government, it is conducted with great ceremony and minuteness of detail, and the only way to obtain a correct view of it is by visiting a respectable theatre during the performance of tragedy such as Chiu shin gura (the forty-seven *rônins*). Here the death of Asano by order of the Shogun, and his follower Hayano Kampei (stage name) by his own hand, in his grief and shame, when falsely accused of the murder and robbery of his own father, give illustrations of the different modes of wiping out a stain on one's honour by means of suicide.

Sometimes a dexterous swordsman severs the head at the moment the abdomen is ripped open, and generally so when the victim is considered by the authorities as guilty of an offence against the Government. In the other case, a friend or faithful retainer may be appointed to this last act of fidelity, to spare the dying man unnecessary and prolonged agony in dying after the self-infliction of the fatal wound. The brave and honest *bushi*, with the small keen stiletto, deliberately rips himself below the navel six inches from right to left and continues the cut for three inches upwards. The cut is not deep, the blade being wrapped in paper, only a small portion of the point being left bare.

---

* *Kuwatzufuku* (Kwapuku) splitting abdomen; but the origin of the name "happy despatch" is obscure. There is no equivalent in Japanese, but under certain circumstances it is looked upon as the correct "finale" to an act of revenge, or stern duty to commit suicide in this way.

The faint-hearted or rebellious or traitorous have the small sword *(tanto* or *ku sun go bu* (.95 of a foot)) laid on a tray in front of them, and when reaching forwards towards it to grasp it, the *kai shak'* (executioner) severs the head from the shoulders, which, in former times, was then placed in a chip box, in the case of an enemy whose head should be brought to his capturers. Of late the friends of the deceased have been allowed to take away the body and the head.

Those culprits who are executed for crime at the execution grounds are beheaded with their hands and arms bound, and the heads are exhibited.

A clever swordsman does not completely sever the head at the first blow, but divides the spine and muscles only, then, grasping the head by the hair and shifting his hold of the sword, he holds the head up, the face towards the official witnesses, and then, at their order, with an upward cut, severs the head and throws it down on the mats. The usual dress on these occasions is a light-blue robe of linen over which a linen *kami shimo* is worn.

Men of rank have silver-gilt screens drawn around them on which white poppy blossoms have been painted. These screens are not therefore in common use, and silver gilding and the white poppy are rarely seen, the combination being suggestive and distasteful, especially in those families any members or ancestors of which have been forced to commit *seppuku*.

Although no longer ordered by the Government, and officially discountenanced, yet of late there have been many cases of *seppuku*. Indeed, within the memory of 'old residents,' cases have occurred of high officers committing *seppuku* because their advice was rejected,—Hori Kura no kami, Hori Oribe no kami, and numbers of others within the last few years of the Tokugawa *régime*. Since then we occasionally hear of the 'death' of an official, but it is looked upon with the same disfavour as duelling is amongst ourselves,—wrong, but sometimes necessary to preserve one's honour.

There are many occasions in which Japanese have died by their own hands, where it is difficult for a foreigner to understand the motive. Such was the case with the two last-mentioned officials, whose sole reason was that their advice was not accepted, and they wished to prove their patriotism and honesty of intention. Again, in some instances there is great dependence placed on the fact that a case of this kind invariably brought on enquiry and notoriety, and the end sought was not unfrequently eventually gained; though the honour comes too late, the family benefits, and the victim attains certain fame.

By way of general remark we may say that suicide was frequently compulsory as a punishment for offending officials. Only under guilty circumstances of a special character and enormity did the family suffer beyond the forfeiture of the income of the suicide. Generally, it was the saving of the family, socially and pecuniarily.

In most instances among men, the act springs—strange to say—from the possession of the very courage, the absence of which may be inferred among ourselves from a similar act, that is, moral courage, which induces them to destroy themselves in order to save their family.

Men and women tired of life who take their future into their own hands are invariably considered insane, under the influence of the fox, or some such power as leads them to harm.

The custom is not by any means disappearing or dying out. The judicial *setzupukku* only is discontinued, and the native papers frequently contain accounts of men ripping open their own abdomens on points of honor or to vindicate their conduct. As in the case of Tsunayoshi's *Midai sama*, the name may be known to posterity as that of a patriotic hero or heroine.

Swords.

The *Katana* (sword) has always been considered the badge of gentle condition in Japan, and has ever been associated in the mind of foreigners with the *yakunin* (official) or the *samurai* (daimio's armed retainer).

The rules of observances connected with the wearing of the long and short sword or the single sword, are most minute, but have fallen into disuse.

Of late the wearing of these weapons is by no means common in the foreign settlements, and even rare in the eastern capital, Tokio. But, in former days, the most trivial breach of these minute observances was often the cause of murderous brawls and dreadful reprisals. To touch another's weapon, or to come into collison with the sheath, was a dire offence, and to enter a friend's house without leaving the sword outside, a breach of friendship. Those whose position justified the accompaniment of an attendant, invariably left the sword in his charge at the entrance, or, if alone, it was usually laid down at the entrance. If removed inside it was invariably done by the host's servants, and then not touched with the bare hand, but with a silk napkin kept for the purpose, and the sword was placed upon a sword-rack in the place of honour near the guest, and treated with all the politeness due to an honoured visitor who would resent a discourtesy. The long sword (if two were worn,) was withdrawn, sheathed, from the girdle with the right hand, and placed on the right side—an indication of friendship, as it could not be drawn and used thus—never by the left hand, or placed on the left side, except when in immediate danger of attack. To exhibit a naked weapon was a gross insult, unless when a gentleman wished to show his friends his collection. To express a wish to see a sword was not usual, unless when a blade of great value was in question, when a request to be shewn it would be a compliment the happy possessor appreciated. The sword would then be handed with the back towards the guest, the edge turned towards the owner and the hilt to the left, the guest wrapping the hilt either in the little silk napkin always carried by gentlemen in their pocket-books, or in a sheet of clean paper. The weapon was drawn from the scabbard and admired inch by inch, but not to the full length unless the owner pressed his guest to do so, when, with much apology, the sword was entirely drawn and held away from the other persons present. After being admired, it would, if apparently necessary, be carefully wiped with a special cloth, sheathed and returned to the owner as before.

The short sword was retained in the girdle, but, at a prolonged visit, both host and guest laid it aside.

Women did not wear swords in their girdles by right or fashion, although when travelling it was often done. On the occasion of fires, the ladies of the Palace sometimes placed side-arms in their girdles.

The ordinary length of the *katana* blade was 2 feet and $\frac{80}{100}$ inches; the small sword, or *wakizashi*, worn with it, 1 ft. $\frac{8}{10}$.

In full dress, the colour of the scabbard was black, with a slight tinge of green or red in it; the binding of the hilt blue silk; the mountings of the guard and hilt *shakudo* (alloy of copper and silver).

The names of makers are innumerable, and each has his particular form of blade, &c. and mode of welding the hard metal of the edge to the softer and tougher body and backing.

Swords more than three centuries old are common enough, and all of later date are called 'new blades' *(shinto)*. Blades made even as far back as the time of our crusades, are to be met with, and there are blades known to be nearly ten centuries old, though these are very rare now. Ama kuni and Shin soku are two of the oldest makers whose swords are still in existence.

Chisakatana is about two feet long to two and a-half feet, and lighter than the ordinary blade, and is worn with the *naga hakama* and the court dress called *daimon* (large crest).

Metezashi (right hand use) is a short sword stuck in the girdle behind, the hilt to the right, used in fighting if the wearer be thrown and unable to draw the swords on the left side of the girdle.

Aikuchi is a short dirk without a guard, worn by doctors, artists, and those with the rank of *Hoin* and *Hogen* (about equal to officials of the fourth and fifth ranks).

Tanto and *mamori katana* are stilettos about a foot long or less, worn in the girdle by officers, gentlemen and nobles, in place of the more cumbrous *wakizashi*.

Jintachi (war-sword); a long heavy two-handed sword, generally carried by a sword-bearer when not in immediate use.

Nodatchi is a sword of medium size, worn when hunting or rambling in country places for pleasure.

Tatchi is hung from the girdle by two slings; there are several styles.

Shin-no-tatchi has a shagreen hilt and on the guard and scabbard and other mountings there should be 75 examples of the crest of the owner.

Yefu notatchi has a lacquered and gilt scabbard.

Sayamaki a portion of the scabbard bound with silk. The mountings are numerous and the making of them is a special and honourable trade. Goto Yujo was a celebrated maker of the 15th century, whose descendants still exist. The work of this family is called *Iyebori* (the families' chasings.)

The first group, called 'articles of three places,' comprises, *first*, the ferule on the head of the hilt, and the ring behind the guard : *second,* the two pieces of metal interwoven with the silk binding of the hilt, used to hide the hole of the rivet, and to ensure a better and firmer grasp of the sword hilt ; and *third,* the small knife and skewer-like pieces of metal inserted into the scabbard so as to be drawn out for use at pleasure. The small knife was used to throw at an enemy ; the skewers to attach the heads of slain enemies to the girdle.

The guard *(tsuba)* is often a wonderful piece of workmanship in metal. *Nanban* (southern iron) was considered the best, but they were often made of valuable metal, and worked up with gold, silver &c., into a detailed picture of battles, hunting or scenery. Nearly every article connected with the sword will be richly inlaid to correspond. Guards are also made of several thicknesses of leather or raw hide called *neritsuba,* Shakudo (copper and silver alloy). *Shibuichi* (one-fourth silver, three-fourths copper.) Silver and gold are used as well as iron.

Seppa are the washers, of which there is one or more above and below the guard, made of flat pieces of metal, brass, silver, or gold.

Habaki is a ferule on the 'forte' of the sword extending about an inch below the guard, made of the same metal as the *seppa.*

Kojiri is the ornamental ferule on the lower end of the scabbard, often very expensively inlaid to match the other mountings.

Kurikata is the small cleat on the scabbard through which the *Sage wo* or silk-cord is rove. This is made of various materials, and generally made with the scabbard.

Saguri is a small hook on the scabbard to prevent the sword slipping too far through the girdle.

Tska ito is the silk cord bound crosswise on the hilt. There are several styles of binding, *maki, dashi me nuki, katatemaki, heomaki* &c. Some swords only have sharkskin hilts without silk, but generally the silk binding is over the skin *(same)*, those pieces having the largest nodules being most valuable.

The sheath or scabbard (*scia*) is made of a wood called *Ho,* generally varnished. Black and dark colours are preferred; gaudy crimson and variegated colours are affected by the old 'swashbucklers.' Leather covers are worn over the handsomely lacquered scabbards; sharkskin ground down, inlaid with shell-work or peculiar kinds of lacquer is sometimes seen on scabbards.

Sage wo is the the long silk cord, of various kinds and colours of sennet, about five feet in length for large swords, half that for the short sword, used to bind up the sleeves preparatory to fighting.

On journeys the gentleman's sword-bearer carried the honoured blade covered with the *Shiki hada,* a swordcase of leather of cloth emblazoned with the owner's crest.

Celebrated Swords and Makers.

Old weapons are frequently presented to Kami shrines, especially those dedicated to Hachiman and Dai Jin Gu.

The following are some of the numberless renowned blades and their forgers.

Ama-kuni of Yamato who lived about A.D. 700 was a celebrated maker. One of his blades is said to have been carried off by a crow during the reign of Kanmu Ten O, A.D. 782, and has since been known by the name of the *Kogarasu maru** (little crow). In A.D. 940 Taira Sadamori became the possessor of this sword, which was drawn by him in the wars with Masakado, who was until lately deified at Kanda, Yedo.

Shin-soku, who lived at Usa no Mia of Buzen, was ordered to forge a blade for the son of the Emperor Heizei Ten O in A.D. 806, and he cut his name on the blade, the first time this was done. There is a legend that Riu Jin† came to his assistance.

Of ninety-nine swords he is said to have made, only eight had his name on them, and the Hachiman shrines

---

* Names were given to swords, as to vessels, horses and other favourite possessions, the commonly used affix *maru* meaning "perfect," in this sense and still used for ships. Formerly even the young sons of nobles were thus styled, as Take chi yo maru, a common title for the heir to the Tokugawa line; as also to castles, such as Hon maru (true perfect) or Nishi maru (west perfect).

† Riu Jin is the same as the Old man living at the bottom of the sea in Riugu (Dragon Shrine) the father of Toyotama hime Hiko quarrelled with his brother, and descending into the depths of the sea became enamoured of Toyo and lived with her in coral caves until she was about to bring forth her child. Hiko then built her a hut on the sea shore, rooofing it with cormorant's wings. Here Fuki was born, and his mother Toyo then became a crocodile and returned to her home in the deep. Hiko having displeased her. She left her sister Tama-yori-himé behind, who married Fukiawasedzu and Jimmu Ten O was their fourth child.

are named as being in possession of most these blades, many of which are now little else than a mass of rust.‡

Ohara Taru daiyu Yasutsuna of Hoki, a cotemporary of Shin-soku, forged a blade which in 947 which was used by Raiko (Minamoto Yorimitzu) to kill Shi ten dôji, a celebrated robber. He dreamed that this sword, then still at the Isô shrine, alone had power to break through the spell of invincibility that surrounded this celebrated robber, who is even now known to children as a ghoul. This sword was placed in the Isé Mia as an offering by Tamura Shogun. Another sword of the same make was likewise placed at Kehi-miojin in Echigo by the Shogûn Toshihito.

Ohara Sane-mori, another maker of celebrated swords, lived at the same time. One of his blades was called *Nuke maru*, from its having flown out of its sheath and destroyed the *Ja* (enormous serpent) that came to swallow up Taira Tadamori, who had laid the weapon sheathed beside his pillow, when lying down to rest. Another blade called *Korgarashi maru*, also in the possession of the Heiki family, was reputed to cause trees to wither if it was laid down touching them.

A.D. 985: Yukihira was another celebrated sword-maker. One of his swords was used by Watanabe, the follower of Yorimitzu (Raiko), to cut off the arm of the Onié§ (ghoul) when sent by Raiko to exterminate the wicked ghouls dragons, *ja* &c.

---

‡ There are some of these old blades in the Exhibition at Tokio, one is marked as valued at 700 *yen.*
§ *Vide* Stories *(Kodomo Banashi).*

A.D. 987. Mune chika, a sword-smith living in Sanjo street, Kiôto, in the province of Yamashiro, made a blade called *Cho maru,* possessed by Gonguro of Kamakura. *Cho maru,* was so called from a *cho* (butterfly) being worked into the 'forte' of the blade. Another was placed in the temple of Fudo son at Echigo, and became the property of Wada Saburozaiemon, who repaired the temple at his own cost. The blade was thereafter called *Fudo maru.*

Another was called *Kogitsune maru* (little fox) from its having been forged by the assistance of Inari (Uga no mitama), when Ichi jo no In (A.D. 887) ordered one of the finest workmanship. The name of the maker, Mune chika, was cut on the obverse, and the name *Kokitsune* on the reverse side *(tska).*

Tomonari of Bizen was a noted sword-maker of the same period.

A.D. 1,004 there lived in Yamashiro Yoshi iye, to whom appeared Sumiyoshi Daimio Jin (of the temple at Osaka) and ordered the best blade that could be welded. When it was finished, the maker was on his way to the temple, as ordered, but while crossing the water he dropped the sword into its depths. A cormorant dived, and finding, flew away with it. Shortly afterwards a new sword was found at the Shrine of Sumi yoshi, which proved to be the lost blade, and it is now called *Wuno maru* (*Wu,* a cormorant.)

A.D. 1186. Gotoba no In was partial to sword-makers,‖ the most celebrated of whom were sent for by him in rotation, as follows :—

1st month, Bizen no Norimune.
2nd „ Bitchiu no Sadatsugu.
3rd „ Bizen Nobufusa.
4th „ Awadaguchi no Kuniyasu.
5th „ Bitchiu no Tsunetsugu.
6th „ Awadaguchi no Kunitomo.
7th „ Bizen no Muneyoshi.
8th „ Bitchiu no Tsuguieyê.
9th „ Bizen no Sukemune.
10th „ Bizen no Yukikuni.
11th „ Bizen no Sukenari.
12th „ Bizen no Sukenobu.

The blades made by Gotoba no In are marked with a chrysanthemum and a stroke beneath, (*kiku ichi mon ji*).

A.D. 1204. Yoshimitzu of Awadaguchi in the province of Yamashiro, commonly known as Toshiro. His make of swords, having cut through a druggist's metal mortar (called *Yagen*), are known as *Yagen Toshiro*.

Rai-taro Kuni-yuki is name of a celebrated maker of this period. In 1248 Kuni-mitzu flourished ; in 1250 Kuni-yoshi. In 1279 Naga-mitzu made a sword, afterwards worn by Iyeyasu, called *Adzuki naga mitzu* from its cutting a bean *(adzuki)* thrown into the air.

Other celebrated makers are :—

A.D. Rai Kuni toshi.
1,293. Shin to go Kuni mitzu.

‖ Many of the Imperial family, and daimios, imitated this Mikado, and patronized amateur and professional sword-making.

1,303. Yuki mitsu of Sagami.
1,319. Sadamune of Sagami.
1,320. Go no Yoshi hiro of Yetchiu.

The last is the most celebrated of these renowned makers. He proudly refused to cut his name on the blades, saying that their superiority would be recognized without this.

A.D. 1322 Mura-masa of Senjiu mura in Isé, commonly spoken of as Senjiu-in Mura-marsa. His swords would, it is said, cut a sheet of paper floating on the stream if the sword were only held in the water to meet the paper. Such was the reputed keenness of these weapons, and so great the desire to test it possessed the owners, that when a fitting opportunity occurred, the Tokugawa government forbade their being worn.¶

In 1326 Masa-mune, the most celebrated of sword-makers, forged some of his best blades, now still in existence. The welding shows a peculiar golden tinge, like forked lightning through a dark cloud. He folded his metal from four sides, beat it out and refolded it in a peculiar manner.

In 1338 three lived in Mino, at the village of Seki Shidzu saburo Kani-uji, a pupil of Masa mune.

In 1362 Okane-mitzu, a celebrated maker of sabres, having more sweep in them than the blades of other makers.

A.D. 1370 Kane-sada was a reputed sword-smith of Seki.

¶ The compiler of these notes possesses one, and has experience of the fear and superstitious reverence evinced by natives of all classes for the swords of this maker.

All swords made since 1570 are called *Shintŝ* (new swords) and the old but inferior blades are included with these. The swords of previous make are called *Kotô* (old swords).

Horikawa Kuni-hiro A.D. 1600 was the best of the new (*Shintô*) makers.

In Setsu (Osaka) Tsuda Echizen no kami Suke-hiro was another maker of about the same period (1624).

Subsequent makers are numerous, but as there are no special legends connected with their blades or particular characteristics pertaining to them, the list of their names is omited here.

The edge of the Japanese sword is tempered separately from the body, by being covered with clay when placed in the fire, and this process brings out the marking peculiar to these swords called *ya-ki ba* (burnt head).

These processes vary and are called ;

Suguha or straight edge: the style of Kuni mitzu.

Hoso suguha, (fine thin) straight edge; the Yamashiro style.

Oomidare, large irregular wavy: the Sagami and Bizen style.

Komidare small irregular wavy-same style.

Choji, like cloves laid side by side: Bizen style.

Jiuka, overlaid petals, like flower petals: Bizen style.

Hitatsura, marked with cloudy spots: Soshiu style.

O Notare, large wavy line; common to all.

Ko Notare, a small wavy line; common to all.

Saka ashi, serrated; principally Bizen.

Gunome or *gonome*, five curves and a straight line alternating: Mino and Seki style.

Sambonsugi, three serrated marks and a straight line alternating.

Niye* are spots on the hard metal of the edge, peculiar to certain makes; and *Niyoie*, cloudings and markings in the welding. The markings on the point, called *boshi*, are of several kinds, denoting the peculiar makes.

All these details must be thoroughly studied by every Japanese gentleman, and *Hon Nami* (experts) were pensioned by the Tokugawa government to teach the "true marks."

The shapes of blades were classed as following:—

Ken, two-edged falchions.

Tatchi, swords with a greater curve.

Katana, the common large sword.

Wakizashi, the ordinary medium blade.

Tanto, the short sword, of late most worn with the *Katana*.

Yoroidoshi, a short thick blade.

Yari, a lance.

Naginata, a large-headed lance.

Unokubi tskuri, (cormorant's-head-shaped) a blade flattened out at the point.

Kamuri otoshi, a small pointed stiletto.

Shobutskuri, like a flag leaf, flat backed.

Hiratskuri, broad shaped.

Iwomune, sloping backed.

---

* Swords are said to retain the stain of human blood, if it is not ground out speedily after the death of the victim.

Hako mune, square backed.

Ogisaki, round pointed.

Kirimono, are grooves or hollows in the blades filled with crimson lacquer or carvings of *Fudô, Marishiten,* (Dragons) and sometimes Bonji (Sanskrit) letters and Chinese characters, such as read "*kimi ban zei,*" ('will cut for ten thousand years'); *ten ka tai hei,* (peace beneath Heaven); *sei shin ho koku* (honest heart and patriotic). Some swords have been engraved with poetry of thirty-one syllables.

The shapes of the haft *(homi* or *nakago)* and the marks there on are aserious study to all true swordsmen.

Yasuri me (file-marks) to keep the hilt from slipping.

Hirayasuri; yokoyasuri; taka no ha; Ya hadzu; are the various styles, each having some peculiarity of the maker.

NAMES OF JAPAN.

Historical, Poetical and Colloquial.

Oya-shima no kuni (Country of the eight great islands); from the legend of the eight islands produced by Isanagi and Isanami.

Shiki Shima (outspread islands); from the fact of their being spread out like the flag stones in a garden.

Isojiro-jima (cliff fortress island); from the resemblacne of the cliffs of the coast to a castellated fortress.

Nichi iki (country of the sun); from the sun rising at its east. *Ni to* (nest of the sun); for the same reason,

Toyoashi-wara-chi-wo-aki-midzuho no kuni (fertile sweet flag plain, fifteen hundred ages, prosperous country.)

Onokoro-jima (consolidated drop); from the story of the *amanosakahoko*—heaven suspended sword—being thrust into the depths of chaos by Isanagi and the dripping particles forming into islands.

Toyohara nakatzu-kuni (between heaven and earth); or coming into existence and suspended between between the *in* and *yó*, male and female principles of Chinese philosophy.

Nansen bushiu (southern country of brave warriors).

Fuso koku. Fuso is the name of a tree that is said to petrify, and therefore the fitting emblem of a country that in the process of ages has become solidified and durable. *Yomogi, a shima* (artemisia island) an allusion to the straight and upward growth of that plant and emblematic of the lofty aspirations of the people.

Tamagaki no uchitsu kuni—the country within the boundaries.

Urayasu no kuni—(country of peaceful shores); from the absence of foreign enemies.

Kuashiboku kitaru no kuni (country ruled by a slender sword); from the smallnesss of the sharp swords in comparison with the unwieldy arms of the warriors of the main land of Asia.

Hodzuma no kuni (beautiful country).

Toyoakitsu (happy dragon fly shaped); from the shape of the group of islands as they appeared on the old maps in form similar to a dragon fly.

Kishi koku (the princesses country); from Tenshoku having been the common ancestress of the nation.

Oyamato no kuni (land of great gentleness); in allusion to the great courtesy and kindness of heart of the people.

Wa koku—or the above altered by the elision of the character Ô (great) and read by the Chinese sound or Koye.

Dai Nihon Koku (great sun source country); as being the source from which the sun was seen to rise daily by the ancient inhabitants of the south-western provinces.

Nihon, or the same abbreviated, from which we learn the common Nifon. The usual term Japan would seem to be derived from the Chinese pronounciation *Jipun* which was modified by the early travellers.

On koku (honourable country); is a newly coined name, used by the natives of late years which furnishes a remarkable instance of a departure from the language of self-abasement which the Japanese employ in allusion to themselves.

Many of these names are rarely used and a few only are to be met with in poetical or literary compositions. *Yamato* is frequently employed in this sense.

Mythological and Legendary.

In addition to the *kami* mentioned *ante* p.80 *et seq.* under the heading Japanese Cosmogony and 93 Religion, the numerous others with whose names legends are associated and who are intimately connected with the more recent legendary lore of the ancient heroes of Japan. They are as follows:

Ame no minaka nushi no kami, who existed before the creation.

Takami musubi no kami is the *kamurogi no mikoto* of the *Sinto Harai* (prayers).

Kami musubi no kami is the *kamuromi no mikoto* of the *Harai*.

Sosanó no mikoto, who had been banished to distant lands, found that his evil reputation had preceded him, and he could not induce people to give him a lodging, and he became an outcast from the habitations of man. At length he found his way to the country of Idzumo and at a place called Hino-kawa-kami, passing through the forest he heard a voice as of one weeping in great distress. Approaching, he saw a young woman who was crying bitterly and with her an old man and woman, who informed *Sosano* that she was the chosen victim for that year's annual sacrifice to *Yamada no orochi*, the eight-headed serpent. He offered to protect her, if they would give her to him in the event of his being victorious to which they all agreed. He then placed eight large tubs full of *saké*, on an elevation, and awaited the serpent's approach. When the monster came for his victim he smelt the *saké* and plunging each of his heads into one of the tubs, he swallowed up the whole of it, and was soon helplessly intoxicated, when he fell an easy prey to *Sosano*, who claimed and took the girl to be his wife. When dividing the monster, his sword was unable to cut through the tail, and splitting it open he found in it a wonderful sword *Murakumo no ken*, so called from the habitation of the serpent being among the ever-clouded heights.

Ten shoko dai jin lived for 200,000 years.

The second in succession *Amano oshi-homi-no-mikoto* who was created from the breath of *Sosano*, and was bestowed by Tenshoko with an existence of 300,000 years.

The third was *Ninigi no Mikoto*, the son of *Oshi homi*, and his mother was *Taka musubi*. He was given the daughter of *Oyama Zumi no kami, Konohana saku yahime*—' the blooming tree.' Charge was given him of Ashiwara-nakatz-kuni (Nipon) by Tenshoku and an existence of 310,000 years. As emblems of his office he had charge of the sacred crystal (*Tama*) mirror (*yada no kagami*) and sword (*ken*). These are the three sacred emblems of office still attached to the Mikado.

The fourth Hikohohodemi-no-mikoto, son of the foregoing pair. He had an elder brother Honosussori-no-mikoto, who went fishing while his brother went hunting on the mountains, where he was successful, while the elder could not suceed in catching fish. They changed places, with the result of both being unable to obtain game or fish. But a large fish had carried away the line and hook from the younger, at which his brother was much enraged. He then made a basket full of hooks and offered them instead of the one lost. But this did not appease his brother's anger, and he betook himself to the beach where he was found in great grief and tribulation by Shiwo-tsutsuo no okina, the old god of the tides, who, when he heard the tale told by the younger brother offered to assist him; and, making a basket in which he placed him, sent him afloat on the waves to search for the missing articles, without which, fearing his brother's wrath, he durst not return. He sank to the depths of the ocean to *Riu Giu*, the dragon's sanctuary. Before the gateway was a lake over which spread the branches of a mighty *katsura-no-ki* (an allusion to the moon) on which he rested. Presently a beautiful woman came forth bearing a crystal vase and going to the well for water, on the surface of which she saw the reflection of Hohodemi perched in the branches above. She flew back and told her father she had seen the reflection of an amazingly beautiful being in the water, and that she looked up and had seen the living original in the branches of the tree over the well Riu Jin, her father, declared it must be a son of the gods, and that they must shew him every attention, and invited him to partake of their hospitality. Wada zumi's (wide-spread seas) daughter Toyotama hime (peerless) called to Hohoemi and invited him to enter, and he told his story. The host promised his assistance and offered his guest a home till the lost fishing tackle was forthcoming. A message was sent to all the fish of the seas charging them to search for it, and, when found, to bring the hook and line. In the mean time a mutual love had grown up between the young people, and, with the consent of the *himé's* father, the pair were united.

Three years passed swiftly and happily away with the young couple, but, at length *Hohodemi* longed to visit his own land, and begged that exertions might be renewed to find the still missiong hook and line. Toyotama had not favoured the search, fearing to lose her lover.

All the fish in the ocean were ordered to assemble, but the *akame* (red-body) (the *Tai*) was not present, having sent in excuse a plea of sickness from an injury to the mouth. Upon searching the *akame*, the missing hook was found in its mouth. Hohodemi, possessed of the article the loss of which had caused his brother's anger, wished to return to appease him, and received as a parting gift from Wadazumi the two jewels that control the ebbing and flowing of the tides; Toyotamahime being *enceinte* was told she must go to his country for the birth of her child, and he should prepare a place by the sea-shore to receive her for that purpose, the roof of which must be of the wings of the cormorant. He was then started off on the back of a crocodile and arrived safely, and immediately presented the recovered hook to his brother, though even this did not appease his rage. Then, taking in his hands the jewel of the flowing tides, he ordered them to rise, and his brother was driven from point to point as the floods rose upon him, till he was fain to entreat his younger brother's pardon, promising to be his slave ever more if saved from drowning.* The tides were then ordered to their usual place, and the building to receive Toyohama was begun; but ere the roofing of wings was completed she arrived upon the spot bringing with her her younger sister. She announced that her time of travail had come, and enjoined Hohohemi not to look upon her in her trouble; but he, in his anxiety for her, disregarded her injunction and had the mortification to behold her changed to the form of a huge crocodile, which

* A strange account of a deluge, worthy of attention.

turned and disappeared in the sea leaving her sister Tama-yori-hime and the child Ugaya-fuki-awasezu-no-mikoto (he that was born under the unfinished roof of cormorant's wings) wrapped in grass,—upon the sea shore. Henceforth the sea became inaccessible to man on account of the sin of Hohodemi, who however lived for 637,892 years.

The fifth from Tensho was Ugaya, and Tamayori became his wife and bore him four sons : he lived 836,042 years. This was the first death—*hodzuru*—the term still used on the decease of a Mikado. His remains were enterred at Wagashirayama in the country of Hiuga.

In the days of Senka Ten O (A. D. 636) there was war with Chosen and fighting going on at Shinran and Minnana. Sate-hiko, the son of Otonomo Kane-mura set sail from Hizen to join the warriors of Japan, and as the vessel which bore him away from his native shores receded from view, his loving wife Sayohime ascended the hill Matzoura to obtain a parting glimpse of her beloved lord and master and to offer up prayers for his safety and speedy return victorious. Such was the intensity of her thoughts and gaze that she became transformed into stone, and ever since Matzoura Sayohime has become an expression for devoted affection.

About A.D. 732 the daughter of the Dai-jin Tan-kai-ko was given in marriage to Gen-so of the To (Tang) dynasty of Kara (China), and the latter sent, amongst other valuable presents, a crystal containing an image of Shaka, the features of which, turned in whatever way, could always be seen and hence called *Men-ko-fu-hat*.

The vessel bearing this precious jewel (*tama*) was wrecked. Tan-kai-ko, anxious to recover such a treasure, went to the fishing village of Shido-no-ura, in Sanuki, in the Island of Sikoku, and there fell in with an *ama* (a female-diver) who became his concubine. She, being a notedly good diver, was confided after a few months by Tan-kai-ko with the story of his loss, and volunteered to risk her life to recover the treasure from the deep, if he would vow to make her yet unborn child, should it prove a male, his heir. Then, fastening a rope of great length round her person and placing a small keen blade in her girdle, she disappeared below the sparkling waves, diving down to Riugu (the Dragon-shrine), where among temples and pagodas built of *Shipo*—seven precious jewels—*gold and silver, she found the *tama* enshrined in a temple guarded by fierce dragons. Unable to find an opportunity of abstracting the prize she saw and sought, it occurred to her that in Riugu dead bodies † were abhorred, and she made a deep incision under her left breast, and then, snatching the the jewel, concealed it there. Then, violently jerking the line attached to her, as a signal to those waiting for her on the shore, she feigned death and was hauled to the abodes of mortals unmolested, to all appearances dead. On an examination of her body the coveted jewel was found, and then her still warm corpse was delivered of a male

---

* The seven jewels are *Sango* (pink coral), *Kohaku* (Amber), *Shako* (Mother-of-pearl), *Ruri* (Emerald), *Meno* (Agate), *Shinju* (Pearls) and *Suisho* (Chrystal): *kin* (Gold) and *gin* (Silver) are both usually included in the term.

† The horror of the gods of the sea for the dead is said to be the cause that the bodies of the drowned invariably float ashore if not speedily devoured by fishes.

child, who, at the age of thirteen became a Dai-jin and was named Fusa-saki. Wishing that due respect should be paid to his mother's memory and that proper funeral rites should be performed over her body, he went to Sanuki, and there, walking on the shore, he met an old woman whose appearance denoted great poverty, and who, accosting him, said she was the spirit of his dead mother. Expressing her joy at his high position she then explained to him the means by which she had recovered the jewel, thereby earning for him the right to be his father's heir, and then vanished. He caused prayers to be celebrated in the temples for the repose of her soul and remained a prosperous man until his death.

At the beginning of the ninth century Ono-no-yori-kase was absent from his mistress for an unusually lengthened period, and she, fearing he had deserted her, drowned herself in the Yodogawa near Otokoyama Kito. He returned but a day too late to save her, and, burying her and erecting a tablet to her memory, daily visited her tomb. Over her grave grew a golden flower that bent its blossoms towards the mourner, but resumed their natural position when he departed; it was a hitherto unknown plant, and he named it Omi-na-meshi (the Maiden's flower). After the period of mourning had expired, he desired to follow her to her home in paradise, where he hoped she had become *Jobutzu* (an angel), by his prayers and by the same path by which she had preceded him, and on the same spot drowned himself.

Tawara Tôda Hide-sato, a celebrated leader of the warriors of the day and ancestor of the Fujiwara family, was an expert archer. Once on a time, about the year A. D. 938 he was journeying through the province of Omi, and near the bridge of Seta was accosted by a lovely woman attired in *jiu-ni-shi-to-ye* (twelve robes and an upper robe, worn by the Imperial ladies) who begged of him as a loyal warrior to protect her from her enemy, who destroyed the produce she raised for the support of her family. He could not but consent, and said that having but one shaft in his quiver, he would go for one or two more and return speedily, when she should conduct him to the lair of her foe. Having returned with his arrows, she conducted him to the mountain of Tonami, and by this time night had overtaken them. Tawara's attention was suddenly directed to what appeared like two moons glaring down from the heights upon him, and, discharging a shaft at one of them, it suddenly faded. He sent another shaft at the other, when it too disappeared; but bethinking himself that this must be the great centipede (*O mukade*) he touched the head of his remaining shaft with his tongue ‡ and with a huge effort sent it at the hideous reptile whose faint outline he could but just perceive. That the swift messenger had gone surely on its errand was immediately apparent, for the struggles of the mortally wounded reptile caused the most horrid noises which were weirdly echoed by the surrounding hills. It proved to have coiled itself seven times round the mountain, such was its great length. The lovely

---

‡ Centipedes abhor human saliva. These insects are said to die if the head is kept wet with saliva; it kills the young ones certainly, hence the allusion to spitting on the arrow-head.

woman expressed her unbounded gratitude and wafted him off to the paradise beneath the surface of the *Omi no midzu Umi* (Lake Biwa), § where, before being sent back to earth once more, were given him to robes of silk, sacks of rice, jars of wine, a sword and a bag of money. These were so enchanted that the silk was endless, neither the rice sacks nor the wine jars could be emptied faster than they would refill themselves, the sword was invincible and the money-bag inexhaustible.

In A. D. 935 at the Kitano no Tenman Gu, the spirit of Sugawara appeared to the *Kannushi* (keeper of the shrine) and told him that henceforth he would watch over the devotees at this place, in testimony whereof one thousand pine-trees should grow around the shrine. This occurred, and the Ten O Murakami hearing of it, ordered that thenceforth the posthumous name of Sugawara Michizane Ten man (heavenly-endowed) should be given the affix *Dai-ji-zai ten-jin* (great fertile heavenly spirit).

Ume waka-maru, the son of Yoshida-no-sho-sho of Kiôto was kidnapped ‖ and carried off to the north, but when arrived at Sumidagawa, where Yedo now stands, the boy, who was about thirteen years old, was so worn out with fatigue and cruel usage that he was abandoned in a ditch. A charitable farmer found him, but he was too far gone to be restored, but lived long enough to give his name and tell

---

§ This lovely creature was the *Ja* (serpent) of Riu gu and supposed to be the same as that deified as Tchikubu Shima no Benten, in Omi.

‖ Kidnapping boys and girls to be sold for the basest purposes was not uncommon; these thieves were called Kado-mukashi.

where to find his friends, and, as a dying wish, asked that a willow ¶ tree should be planted on the mound over his grave. A year after, to a day, his mother arrived on the spot, and the spirit of her lost child appeared from the tree: then, after mutual explanations, joined with prayer for the peaceful rest of his spirit *(jobutzu)*, it disappeared.

In the temple-grounds of Mokuboji at Mukojima (a suburb of Yedo) on the banks of the Sumida may yet be seen the tree on the grave.

Raiko (Minamoto Yorimitzu) went hunting in the forests of Sagami. At Ashigara yama he met a boy in a lonely spot who had round him a number of wild animals, evidently on very friendly terms, and was at the moment amusing himself by wrestling with a young bear. The lad conducted him to where he saw a woman, the boy's mother, who appeared to have once possessed great beauty. He was desirous to obtain the boy who showed so much courage, in order to adopt him, but succeeded only by allowing the mother to accompany them. It subsequently turned out that she, since known as Yamauba (old woman of the hills), had been the wife of Sakata no Toki yuki, a warrior of the Genji party, and when he died the mother and child fled to the hills of refuge from their enemies. The father is known in children's stories as Kintaro, the son as Kintoki; and common pictures represent him in company with his mother and beasts of the forest. He afterwards became

¶ Willows are very commonly planted over graves as emblems of the grief of the departed, in strange contradistinction to our idea of them as betokening the weeping of the sorrowing relations.

known as Sakata Kintoki and a famous warrior. This occurred about A. D. 1,004.

Several years afterwards the Ten O Ichi-jo ordered Raiko to subdue the wicked *Shui ten do ji*, the ghouls that appeared at the *Ra-sho-mon* and also *Tsuchi gume*. He took with him the four strongest of his followers, first of whom was Kintoki, the others being Watanabe, Usuie and Urabe. Their adventures form the foundation of numerous legends.

About 1084 a priest named Rai go ajari died, and it is related that his spirit transmigrated into a rat, and that the vermin went to Kiôto and eat or destroyed all the prayer-books and other temple furniture of Hiyesan.

Taira Kore mochi of the Heike family went to Taka o san for pastime to view the maple trees. He saw a group of maidens pic-nicing, and, dismounting from his horse, would fain have passed without alarming or disturbing the fair nymphs. But the queen of the party ordered him to be invited to join them, and he, nothing loth, accepted the wine-cup, which had but just been touched by her own sweet lips, from her fair hands. What with the wine he drank and the feminine charms around him, he soon became fairly intoxicated and went off to sleep, but he was aroused by the violent trembling of the earth to see before him a gigantic *Oni* who was fain to devour him. But quicker than thought, the trusty steel was drawn from its sheath as he bounded erect, and, almost with the same spring, reached the ghoul and slew him.

www.ingramcontent.com/pod-product-compliance
Lightning Source LLC
Chambersburg PA
CBHW020826190426
43197CB00037B/715